The Collector's Encyclopedia of
CARNIVAL GLASS

BY
Sherman Hand

Copyright: Bill Schroeder, Sherman Hand, 1978

ISBN 0-89145-071-8

*Additional copies of this book along with current value
guide may be ordered @ $19.95 postpaid from:*

COLLECTOR BOOKS
Box 3009   Paducah, Kentucky   42001

TABLE OF CONTENTS

FOREWORD

To set the stage, perhaps I should tell you the iridescent glass which so successfully took the whole country by storm — twice — was not called Carnival Glass in the beginning. There were several companies which made iridescent glass, and there were as many names for the glass as there were companies which made it. The Fenton Art Glass Company called theirs Aurora; Northwood called his Regna; Imperial Glass Company used Sunset Hues for their iridescent glass; and the Millersburg Glass Company called theirs Rodium Ware.

I am sure you have heard stories of Carnival Glass being made to compete with Tiffany, Aurene, Steuben, and other iridescent glass. I don't think Mr. Fenton had any ideas of competing with those companies because of their limited success with iridescent art glass. It was limited success because of the expensive process of making it, and only the very rich could afford it. Fenton didn't want a limited success; he wanted a product which would establish him and his new company. He got just that when he devised a method of applying the iridescence to the outside of the glass instead of mixing it in the glass itself. It was a much cheaper process, just as effective, and a lot more successful.

Let's take a look at some of the companies which made Carnival Glass, beginning with the Fenton Art Glass Company and Mr. Fenton, who pioneered the process.

The Fenton Art Glass Company

Before the age of 20, Frank L. Fenton had been a glass worker, glass decorator, and a factory foreman in fine glass houses, including Northwood.

As he became more proficient in glass decorating, he began to wonder if his designs would sell on other people's glass, why not start his glass company? He approached his older brother, John W. Fenton, whose talents lay in organization and business promotion, and suggested they go into business.

With under $300, the Fentons founded their first glass company at an old factory site in Martin's Ferry, Ohio. They first bought blank glass and put their original designs on them. When their work became popular, the company supplying their blanks became worried because the Fentons were making inroads in their business, so they limited the supply.

The Fentons heard of a factory site for sale in Williamstown, West Virginia, and with John's business acumen, they purchased a block of land, sold lots and raised the necessary capital to build the factory. On January 2, 1907, the first piece of glass was made at the Fenton Art Glass Company.

Not long after, the first of the iridescent glass now known as Carnival was made, and soon the Fenton Art Glass Company was a booming success.

Despite the company's prosperity, Frank Fenton remained a designer and artisan. He loved to create new patterns. Some of his most famous patterns were the Horse Medallion, Butterfly and Berry, Butterfly and Fern, Orange Tree, Dragon and Lotus. He probably was responsible too for Little Fishes and the Peter Rabbit Bowl, although there were undoubtedly others who had a hand in some of the designs.

One of these was a Fenton moldmaker, J. Frank Smith, who worked for the Fenton Art Glass Company from 1913 to 1917. Smith is credited with the Heavy Grape pattern. He is said to have hung a big bunch of grapes in front of him while cutting the mold. Smith is also believed to be the originator of the famous Parkersburg Elk plate or bowl (a Fenton product), since he was a member of the Grand Order of Elks, and supposedly attended at Parkersburg.

Collectors of fine glass would have missed much if Frank Fenton had not created the Carnival Glass field and founded factories like the Fenton Art Glass Company. It is difficult for this author to imagine not being able to appreciate this beautiful glass. A century from now, glass collectors will still be inspired by Carnival pieces.

Northwood Glass Company

Harry Northwood was the son of John Northwood, who was a famous glass maker in England. He migrated to the United States and worked with some of the finest glass companies and artisans this country had to offer. After some time, he purchased the old Hobbs, Brockunier plant known as the Wheeling Glass Works and produced some of the finest art glass available. Later he bought several other glass companies which were near bankruptcy around the turn of the century during the glass recession.

Mr. Northwood found a piece of glass that one of his former employees was offering for sale which looked very promising. He purchased a piece of this new glass being produced at the Fenton Art Glass Company and shipped it to his father in England to have him analyze the coating on the outside of the glass. After much tedious work, Harry's brother, John Northwood II, isolated the material and found it to be chloride of iron.

Apparently Mr. Northwood's first attempts were not successful, but being a master craftsman, he overcame the problems and was soon producing fine iridescent glass. In fact, he overshadowed the Fenton Art Glass Company to some extent because he was better known, owned several plants and was associated with others. Actually, Mr. Northwood produced the lion's share of Carnival Glass and today is considered famous for some outstanding rare patterns, such as the Farm Yard, Morning Glory, Hobnail, Wishbone, and others, and for his ice-blue, ice-green, and aqua-opalescent colors. Yet, after all is said and done, Grape and Cable was THE pattern and marigold THE color. This was the pattern and the color which outsold all the others.

The Imperial Glass Company

Unfortunately, we don't have the data as to how the Imperial Glass Company got the formula for Carnival Glass, though we assume it was much the same story as Northwood's — by isolating the material. At least, they got it and were soon making a lot of beautiful glass. Imperial was known for the patterns Luster Rose and Open Rose. They made many of the near-cut patterns, and their Nu-Art plates are highly collectible and expensive.

Imperial made some of the finest purple we find today, but for some reason they didn't make as much purple as some of the other companies, seeming to favor marigold and green. They made very little red in Carnival, but did make quite a bit of red in Stretch Glass, which is a second cousin to Carnival Glass and is gaining in popularity at this time.

Though space doesn't allow the history of all the glass companies which were involved in making Carnival Glass, I think we should give at least some history about the Millersburg Glass Company, which was the shortest-lived, but probably the most colorful, of the four major glass companies which produced Carnival Glass.

Millersburg Glass Company

The Millersburg Glass Company was founded by John Fenton and his brother Robert. After the closing of the Millersburg plant, Robert returned to Williamstown and worked at the Fenton Art Glass Company. It is believed he took some of the molds from the Millersburg plant with him. John Fenton chose to stay on in Millersburg after the closing of the plant.

John Fenton had worked as a streetcar conductor in Wheeling, West Virginia, until he quit to help his brother Frank found the Fenton Art Glass Company. John, with this fresh taste of victory after being so successful in helping found that company, decided to start a glass factory with Robert and they began to search for a site. During their quest for a location, they chanced into Millersburg, Ohio. They liked the Amish people, the rolling hills and the beautiful Killbuck river valley. It was a farming community, serviced by a railroad.

Millersburg had not been among the plant sites that the Fentons set out to examine. There was sand in the county, but coal was not being mined in the immediate vicinity. There were no suitable buildings available, nor was there an abundant supply of labor, skilled or unskilled. Nevertheless, there was much in the community to please the brothers. There was an available parcel of land on the northwest side of town, and there was an avid interest expressed by the citizens in providing money with which to purchase the land.

More delightful was the enthusiasm with which the stock of the proposed company was received. It was first offered at $100 per share, and the initial offering was over-subscribed. The price quickly went as high as $145 per share as an indication of the confidence felt by the citizenry. Bear in mind that this was 1908, and visualize what $100 would mean to a conservative farmer of that era.

With money in the bank, plans for the building were drawn. It was the first building in the world to span 100 feet without interior supports. The chimney was 60 feet across at the base, 30 feet across at the top, and 125 feet tall. The Fentons purchased the iron girders for the shop at the World's Fair in Chicago, and there was considerable excitement in the small town when the railroad cars carrying the girders arrived.

The Fairbanks Morse Company in Cleveland designed and built an 80-horsepower engine for $6,000. Another major item was a converter which consumed coal to create gas, which is an easily controlled heat source. The coke, or ashy residue from the burned coal, was sold to the Hinkley Foundry which was to cast the molds.

By early 1909, according to the "Holmes County Farmer," workmen were installing the machinery, dynamos, and wiring which were to make this the best equipped glass plant in the world.

The Fentons hired Oliver Phillips and his three sons from Findlay, Ohio, to organize the crew and oversee the details of preparing for the first pour or gather. Experienced glass men were recruited from nearby states, some mold makers were brought from Germany and other European glass centers. Robert Fenton created most of the designs.

Apparently, the new company started with three patterns: the Peacock, the Grape, and the Maple Leaf. The first colors were amethyst ruby (which we call marigold), crystal or clear, and milk glass, which probably is what we call peach-opalescent. The products advertised as iridescent art glass also were known as Rhodium Ware.

The first big display of Millersburg glass was at Pittsburgh and it was an immediate success. Viewers described it as "pulsating with life", and its fame spread throughout the world. Hawaii received its share of the glass. Germany, France, and England, glass centers themselves, took to the iridescence or to the patterns and some Millersburg pieces found their way into the possession of King Edward VII of England.

So rapidly did the glass gain popularity that the factory soon employed two 12-hour shifts. Fourteen tons of glass were processed during each day's run. The wage scale for the average factory worker was $1.50 per 12-hour shift.

The Fentons soon realized that converting coal to gas was an expensive source of heat. This prompted a wildcat well-drilling south of town, and the first probe became a producing well. Employees donated their time to lay pipe from the well to the factory, and it is thought that these acts caused Robert Fenton to design and cast the Millersburg Courthouse bowl and plate. They were a means of demonstrating appreciation to the community.

From all accounts, every factory worker, every stockholder, and everyone who donated to purchase the land was given a set. No doubt, there were others. The mystery today is what happened to the bulk of these once plentiful items.

In another expression to his faithful employees, Mr. Fenton designed and cast the Christmas Compote. It is a large open compote with the Holly Leaf pattern, similar to the Holly Whirl. However, it has a larger foot than most compotes and the stem was almost eliminated. The only colors, apparently, were amethyst, green, and marigold. Mr. Fenton determined that the iridescent quality of each set was excellent. The beautiful pieces were presented at a company Christmas party and these, too, have become extremely hard to find.

Today, the residents of Millersburg are very proud of their glass heritage. A visitor is given to understand that their iridized glass is not "Carnival". To them, it has always been "Millersburg Glass", definitely an art glass, and they want to keep it that way. Many homes have fine examples of the product. The Court House design is seen often. Of exceptional interest is a Hobstar and Feather punchbowl with 12 cups, and one of todays' fastest rising rarities is the Cleveland Ashtray.

The Millersburg Glass Company closed its doors early in 1914. Some say that the stiff competition caused the small producer to fail. Some say that "cheap reproductions" ruined the market.

The original plant still stands, occupied by another manufacturer. The old stack has been destroyed, the machinery dismantled, and the molds and patterns scattered or demolished. Otherwise, all that is left of the glass era are a few dumps where pieces of broken casts can be unearthed. Some of these help to confirm or deny origins of some specimens. There are a few residents who experienced the glass period and are a source of valuable information, but none say they never dreamed the glass in their possession would command the attention it is now receiving.

Strange as it seems, the closing of the Millersburg plant had little affect, if any, on the Carnival Glass market. All the other companies were working full time, some overtime, making glass and selling it all over the world. This went on into the early Twenties, which was unheard of for one type of glass. Four to six years was the normal life, and ten years was considered a long run for any glass before housewives rebelled and refused to buy.

This iridescent glass lasted fifteen years, which had never been done before, and, at the time of this writing, has not been duplicated. But at last, housewives did rebel and wanted another type of glass. The glass companies were stuck with warehouses full of iridescent glass, so they unloaded it on cut-rate houses, shows, and some of it was given away at carnivals.

Someone thought of the name "Carnival Glass" and the name stuck, which I think is very appropriate. When I think of carnivals, I think of colors, gaiety, and excitement — just what I have found while collecting this glass which has no peers. I have been associated with glass for many years and know of no other glass which has taken the country and most of the world by storm twice.

Patterns, Pieces, and Colors

I'm sure you can appreciate the fact that it is impossible to show every piece or pattern made in Carnival Glass, but we have compiled the biggest collection of pieces, patterns, color, and information ever offered for this type of glass. We have made every effort to show something for everybody, from the amateur to the advanced collector. If we have succeeded, we are happy because this is what we had in mind when we started this project.

We have not shown all pieces and patterns, but have tried to show representative items.

Colors can be most helpful in identifying the manufacturer of a certain piece, which is especially important in some cases. Fenton made the bulk of the red; Northwood made most of the ice-green, ice-blue, and the aqua-opalescent; Imperial made the bulk of the smoke, which we did not show because it is too difficult to photograph and reproduce its true color, and the best in purple; Millersburg probably made the best true amethyst (not a purple). Millersburg products also have a finer textured iridescence with a little more shiny look.

White pieces should be a frosty white, not clear. The red should be a cherry red, not an over-balanced amethyst. Red is considered rare in Carnival Glass because it is a difficult color, even in the old pressed glass. The color usually burned out and just was not a good true color, so it has always been scarce. Fenton had the best luck with red; Imperial did fairly well, but not well enough to make a lot of it. Perhaps that is the reason we don't find more of the red today.

Before Carnival Glass came on the scene, there had been an opalescent glass period. Housewives had bought it for years and were tired of it, so when the glass companies tried to introduce aqua-opalescent Carnival Glass, perhaps the housewives thought they were just iridizing the old stuff they had on hand because the aqua-opalescent did not do well.

Rarities

In most cases, a rarity is a piece or pieces, pattern, color, or shape that is desirable and the demand is much greater than the supply. Why didn't the companies make an equal amount of this type of glass? There are as many reasons as there are rare pieces. In many cases, the pieces did not come out of the mold right and the breakage was high. Other pieces and patterns just did not appeal to the trade, and, if something didn't sell well, it was scrapped right away. They were in business to make money so they made the things which sold the best.

We are often asked if items are valuable because they are rare. The answer is "Not necessarily". First, an item has to be desirable. There are some pieces which are probably one-of-a-kind, yet they are practically worthless. Others are worth thousands of dollars in today's market.

Does a chip or heat check affect the price of an item? It affects the price just whatever you think it does. If you think it is five dollars, then it is five dollars. If you think it is more, then it is.

I have written before that if something is worth collecting, it is worth reproducing. There will be more reproductions, and they will get better. We have mentioned many reproductions in this book, and before it is finished there will be more, but if you study your glass you won't be misled.

My apologies to the veteran collector if I have repeated myself from some of my other books or articles, but as new collectors are still joining our ranks, I felt it was absolutely necessary. I would like to take this opportunity to thank our many friends in the Carnival Glass field for their help and encouragement. Good luck and good hunting.

DEDICATION AND ACKNOWLEDGEMENTS

I would like to dedicate this book to Mr. and Mrs. F. M. Whitley of Houston, Texas who have been very generous in contributing to this book with their time, effort, encouragement, the loan of their pieces and their enthusiasm in promoting Carnival Glass.

I would also like to give special thanks to Connie and Don Moore who opened their home to us and were so generous with their time and information, and their untiring work of getting the glass for me to photograph and then putting it away again.

My appreciation also goes to Charlotte and Gordon Williams of Galt, California who provided many pieces of their collection.

For some of the rarities, I would like to thank the Roebucks of Elizabeth City, North Carolina.

And to the many people who helped me in other books, again my thanks. Most of all, to the collectors and the dealers who made my other books a success, thank you.

A very special thanks to my loving wife, Timme, who put in so many hours helping me carry my photographic equipment many places and helping me photograph, plus the typing, cataloging, collating and many other jobs beyond the call of duty. Most of all, her faith and encouragement were with me all the way.

GRAPE AND CABLE MASTER PUNCH SET

Northwood made three different sizes of the Grape and Cable punch sets. This one, of course, being the largest one. The smallest or regular size measures only about 11″ across the top, and the middle size one about 14″ across the top, while this particular one measures 17″ across the top. (See inset though I doubt you could find one for that price!) These we believe were made for banquets and other gala events, but we think it is quite unique that we find these in such a variety of colors. There are marigold, amethyst, cobalt blue, green, ice blue, ice green and white. We have seen cups in aqua-opalescent, and since the cups are all of one size, will some day a master punch bowl turn up in aqua-opalescent?

FLUTE PUNCH SET

This simple pattern was used very extensively by several companies, mostly as a secondary pattern. This is the Imperial Glass Company's set. They also made a water set and a four piece table set. Northwood did also, though Northwood marked almost all of his with an N. The Imperial Company very seldom marked any of their Carnival glass, and when they did it was marked with the old Iron Cross. But this set would hardly need marking, because Imperial made some of the finest purple ever made, and this is one that will prove it.

THE "LITTLEST" PUNCH BOWL

This really isn't a punch bowl. In all probability it was used for sauce or perhaps gravy and even mayonnaise. By calling it a punch bowl, however, I can indulge myself in a wisp of humor showing it with the jumbo bowl and laying claim to the biggest and the littlest punch bowls. It's usually good for a laugh or a chuckle all around. There is no pattern and the iridescence is of poor quality. No marks are visible so we do not know the manufacturer.

SECTION 1 — PUNCH SETS

EXTRA LARGE IRIDESCENT PUNCH SET.

AO2142—Height 14 inches, width 16 inches, raised grape pattern, wine ruby iridescent effect, fancy crimped and scalloped top, detachable foot; set consists of 1 punch bowl and foot, 12 cups and hooks; 1 set in barrel, set, **$3.75**

Grape and Cable Master Punch Set

Flute Punch Set

"Littlest" Punch Bowl

MULTIFRUITS AND FLOWERS PUNCH SET

I encountered this lovely set in a home near Millersburg, Ohio. It had been a family heirloom, purchased in the factory-community many years ago, and I am grateful many times over that they would consent to part with it.

This particular set had 12 cups as did other sets that were owned nearby. There were three colors in evidence, marigold, amethyst and some green that was unearthed in fragments.

The base can be readily mistaken for a compote and may have been sold alone, in many instances, for that purpose.

THE MULTIFRUITS PUNCH SET

This is a feature item for any book or collection. It has so many distinctive characteristics. The base has a much larger collar base for the bowl to sit on making it more sturdy, and instead of being round it is eight-sided, which makes it look more attractive. Also the base is iridized on the inside so it could be turned upside down and make a lovely compote. Note the assemblage of grapes, cherries and pineapple — and the pineapple is upright. The cups that accompany this set are very dainty and carry the same pattern — less the scallops of course. These are rather rare in any color, possibly more of them in amethyst or marigold, but not many known in any color. This is a Millersburg product, probably made shortly before the plant closed, and is in the collection of the author.

Multifruits and Flowers Punch Set

The Multifruits Punch Set

S REPEAT PUNCH SET

This is another one of the master or banquet punchbowls about the same size as the Grape and Cable. This one is definitely in the scarce category because I have seen only three or four. Shown here in amethyst, and what few I have seen have been in amethyst, though it is always possible some will show up in other colors — maybe other pieces. So far, the punch bowl and cups and a tooth-pick are the only pieces that I know of in this pattern. There are numerous tooth-picks in this pattern, but most, if not all of them, are new. We have no way of tracing the manufacturer of these pieces. Some of the old pressed glass companies used this pattern, mostly on cruets and small pieces, but we can't associate those companies with Carnival glass.

S Repeat Punch Set

ROSE WREATH PUNCH SET
Grape Interior Pattern

This Rose Wreath punchbowl comes in two different ways. The one shown here has grapes on the inside, while the other version has the Persian Medallion pattern on the inside. The cups also have the grapes inside (not shown here), while the cups for the other version have the Persian Medallion inside. Usually this bowl is shaped differently — not flattened out so much and higher and not so wide across the top. We just chose this because of its odd shape. This is a Fenton product.

ROSE WREATH PUNCH SET
Persian Medallion Interior Pattern

This Rose Wreath, we think, can definitely associate with Fenton because the inside of the bowl has the Persian Medallion pattern, which we know was made by the Fenton company, while the other Rose Wreath punch set has the Grape pattern on the inside. Some well known authorities think these may have made by two different companies. Whichever the case may be, both sets are nice and both are desirable, and are in the collection of Don and Connie Moore.

Rose Wreath Punch Set — Grape Interior Pattern

Rose Wreath Punch Set — Persian Medallion Interior Pattern

FOUR SEVENTY FOUR PUNCH SET

I think this punch set in purple shows Imperial at its finest. This pattern was used more on punch sets than anything else and was made by the ton in marigold, but limited very much in purple. Today this set in purple is rather rare and is almost as hard to find in green as it is in purple. This is from the fine collection of the Moores.

PERSIAN GARDEN TWO PIECE FRUIT BOWL

Fruit bowls and Punch bowls can be confusing, especially in the two-piece presentations.

The dimensions of this one (10" across top, 7½" high) together with the fact that I have never seen punch cups led to the identification. The base might be used as a candy dish by upending it. Iridescence was applied to the inside, apparently to give it this added usefulness.

Of course, this is typically a Fenton product. The basket weave effect outside, the Persian Garden pattern inside and the beautiful purple testify to that. It may have been made in other colors.

Four Seventy Four Punch Set

Persian Garden Two Piece Fruit Bowl

THE MEMPHIS PUNCH BOWL SET

This beauty is often called the Aristocrat of the punch bowls and one could readily guess that it is a Northwood product, even if it was not marked (N).

This signature, incidentally, appears on all the punch bowls and cups that I have seen.

How this pattern got its name is a mystery. One can only speculate that it could have been inspired by some exquisite artifact unearthed at the site of Memphis, the early capital of Egypt.

In old catalogs, the design is listed as a near-cut, but that description could fit many glass patterns.

This bowl was made in several colors.

BROKEN ARCHES PUNCH SET

The Broken Arches punch set is probably not as rare as the Grape and Cable or S Repeat Banquet sized punchbowls, but we feel that the color and the exceptional iridescence warrant a place in the history of glass. This set is unmarked but we feel sure this was made by the Imperial Glass Company.

Memphis Punch Set

Broken Arches Punch Set

INVERTED FEATHER PUNCHBOWL

This is undoubtedly a rare punchbowl. It is the regular size. We wonder why we find so few pieces with this pattern. There must have been cups with this punchbowl, but for some reason they became separated. The cracker jar with this pattern may be found rather handily, and there is a milk pitcher, shown elsewhere in this book. Like most of the cracker jars, the punchbowl does have the near-cut mark. Thanks to Connie and Don Moore for the loan of this piece.

THE MANY FRUITS PUNCH SET

This bowl is unmarked, yet we know this to be Northwood's pattern. The Northwood Peach is displayed as is the Northwood Grape. Inside and on the base is the Northwood Cherry.

This could have been called the "Many Ways" Punch Bowl. Alone, the bowl can be used for fruit. Overturn the base and it will serve as a beautiful open compote since iridescence is on the underside and the cherry pattern on the outside.

There are six cups. The grapes, far different than either Grape and Cable or Northwood Vintage, match those on the bowl.

The bowl may be found in two conformations, scalloped and ruffled, and at least two colors, purple and marigold, although it has been reported in green.

Inverted Feather Punch Bowl

Many Fruits Punch Set

HOB STAR AND FEATHER PUNCH SET

This is a double rarity. This tulip shape is something not often encountered in a punchbowl — a rose bowl, yes; a punchbowl, no. This would be about a standard size punchbowl, near 12 inches, if the top wasn't crimped in. This is Millersburg at its best. These are scarce in any color, but to find one with the color and iridescence of this one is a collector's dream come true. Again our thanks to lucky Don and Connie Moore for the loan of this piece.

ACORN BURR PUNCH SET

This set was made by Northwood and it has proven to be a collector's favorite. It came in all the colors including ice green, ice blue and aqua-opalescent; the marigold and amethyst are found more often than the green. When I started to photograph this punch set I couldn't decide which I liked best — the pup or the punch bowl so I sat the pup in the punchbowl and snapped the camera. (Note: The little inset from the old catalog — 1912 Baltimore Bargain Book — new Raised Chestnut pattern.) Our many thanks to Charlotte and Gordon Williams for the loan of the punchbowl and the puppy.

IRIDESCENT GLASS PUNCH BOWL AND FOOT.

AO2140—Height 11 inches, width 11 in., new chestnut raised pattern; assorted colors, green, golden iris and wine ruby iridescent effect; total, 3 in barrel...each, **95c**

Hob Star and Feather Punch Set

Acorn Burr Punch Set

23

ORIENTAL POPPY WATER SET

The Oriental Poppy, a Northwood pattern, is a highly collectible grouping with well-executed pattern throughout the several pieces (it was occasionally sold with only four tumblers).

The set is shown here in purple but it appeared in a number of other colors, including white. It is very attractive in ice green.

Perhaps the most unusual aspect is that the tumblers have the (N) mark but the pitcher doesn't. As a rule the big piece was marked and the smaller ones not.

PANELLED DANDELION WATER SET

This popular water set was made in all the usual colors. However, the cobalt blue must have been the color preferred when they were made, because we find more of them in blue. Not many are found in marigold, and the amethyst is not plentiful. Green seems much scarcer and the white is almost impossible to find. We wonder sometimes why, because Fenton made a lot of white. These are still available, at least in some of the colors. Whichever color you find, I am sure you will enjoy it.

SECTION 2 — WATER SETS

Oriental Poppy
Water Set

Panelled Dandelion
Water Set

THE DOUBLE STAR WATER SET

On the bottom of this pitcher is the Near Cut mark but it is absent from the tumblers.

Like the Inverted Thistle and Inverted Strawberry, this is a difficult set to find, obviously because small quantities were produced.

Although no fragments were found at Millersburg, the fantastic iridescence is identical to that company's and the amethyst coloring is characteristic of its best. This is heavy, fine quality glass.

BLUEBERRY WATER SET

If you like blueberries, you will especially enjoy this design, especially the tumblers. Held to the light, the berries appear to be just off the vine and the cobalt blue is just the right color to give them realism.

Fenton also made this in marigold and white and perhaps green.

LEMONADE AND WATER SETS.

The Blue Berry Water Set is included in the offerings from Rouss Monthly Catalog issued in March, 1914.

ZF5539. "Money's Worth." Three entirely new shapes and designs—fruit, orange blossoms and berry embossings; royal blue and pearl iridescent. Eeach set consists of one full ½-gallon jug with stuck handle and six full size tumblers to match; 6 sets to bbl....SET, .55 Shipped from Depot F.

Double Star Water Set

Blueberry Water Set

HEAVY IRIS WATER SET

This water set is harder to come by than most, yet so desirable that we wish there was one for every collection. Shown here in amethyst, which is choice over the marigold, and is far from easy to obtain. The white is next to impossible to find. All the information we have indicates they had trouble with this mould for the pitcher. Note, if you have one available, that the sides of the pitcher are thin — about half the thickness of the other water pitchers. The pattern is very predominant or stands out quite thick. Also note this is a tall tankard type pitcher, and most of them have what we call a "fold" in the glass. It looks like a wrinkle in the glass in the bottom of the pitcher. To me this indicates mould trouble. For that reason we think these had a short run. There was no trouble with the tumblers. Every tumbler collector from Texas to Nome has 3 or 4, but how many pitchers do you find?

SPRINGTIME WATER SET

Here is a set that has nearly disappeared from the open market, especially in the dark hue.

The set was shown in the trade catalogs in 1912. Apparently, it did not enjoy the popularity of the Massive Grape (which we now call Grape and Cable).

The pitcher and tumblers all carry the famous (N) and were made in all the usual Northwood colors.

Heavy Iris Water Set

Springtime Water Set

CHERRY WREATH WATER SET

This is one of the patterns that the Diamond Glass Company used before Northwood purchased the Diamond Glass plant. Apparently he used this pattern for a while, and a few of the butter dishes got through with the old Diamond mark in the bottom — the letter D inside a diamond. But I guess Mr. Northwood didn't like making glass with someone else's name on it, so he soon stopped that. This set was made in all the colors but the marigold is usually hard to find. Still harder to find is the white one with the painted cherries.

THE FLUFFY PEACOCK

This set is far different from the Millersburg Peacock with which all collectors are familiar.

In this artist's version, there are some points for dispute but it is still exceptional. One might assume that this was designed by Robert Fenton during his association with the Millersburg factory.

Cherry Wreath Water Set

The Fluffy Peacock

BOUQUET WATER SET

We have done considerable research on this particular water set and came up with a blank. Again you don't see it too often. The color and iridescence is far different from that usually found on sets made by bigger companies that made Carnival Glass. We think it may have been done by one of the small companies not so well known that did some fine work and didn't get much publicity. We think this set would enhance almost any collection.

FASHION WATER SET

This is one of the near-cut patterns made by the Imperial Glass Company. There have been reissues of this pattern in tooth picks, etc., but I have not seen the pattern in water sets. It has exceptional color and iridescence. It is shown here in marigold, but I could add that it would be a collector's dream to find this set in purple.

Bouquet Water Set

Fashion Water Set

GRAPE ARBOR WATER SET

This water set is shown here in ice-blue, perhaps the most common color except marigold. Probably it is a toss-up between them for availability, with the white being next. The amethyst is very difficult to find, and the ice-green very rare. Being a bulbous type tankard pitcher with the high raised grapes and the glass thinner than some of the others, it became very vulnerable to breakage. We find quite a few with folds in the glass in the bottom, which might indicate mould trouble in the making. Also, the tumblers did not fare any better, with their wide base — they seemed to always get chipped. These sets are so beautiful, we believe they were made in mass quantities, but just didn't fare so well. This is a Northwood product and almost all the tumblers carry the N in the bottom.

TEN MUMS WATER SET

This set is definitely on the scarce side. How many are around we don't know, but I believe I could find more God and Home water sets than I could these. Usually when you find one it is blue. Occasionally you may find one in marigold, but rarely in amethyst or green. And again, the white one is the difficult one to find, though we have seen it in white. We have seen this set advertised in the old catalogs grouped with other known Fenton patterns, and we think more than likely this is a Fenton product.

Grape Arbor Water Set

Ten Mums Water Set

MAPLE LEAF WATER SET

This water set probably came in all colors, but it is most often found in either amethyst or marigold, and is a very attractive set. I don't recall seeing any of these pitchers or tumblers with an N on it, however it has been attributed to Northwood. This set has been reissued or reproduced, probably by Westmoreland Glass Company and should be marked, they tell me. Anyway, I think a novice collector could distinguish the difference, even though the reproductions are getting better.

GRAPE AND LATTICE WATER SET

This water set, shown here in a typical Fenton cobalt blue, also was popular in marigold. It is seldom seen in green or amethyst. We have encountered a few in white, though they are by no means plentiful. The grape pattern has been popular for many years. The tankard pitcher takes a mite less room than the bulbous pitchers, and a little space saved could mean room for another piece of Carnival for display. But whether you are conserving space or not, the odds are that you would appreciate this lovely set.

Maple Leaf Water Set

Grape and Lattice Water Set

CRAB-CLAW WATER SET

This pattern shown here is probably like some of the other Imperial Glass Company near-cut patterns that did not fare so well, like the Royalty and a couple of others that were very graceful. Yet, for some unknown reason, there seems to be such a few of these beautiful pieces. This is a well executed pattern, maybe a little busy, yet very attractive. So far these sets have been reported or seen only in Marigold. Are there other colors? Time will tell. I am sure there are tumbler collectors who would like to find one in another color.

BUTTERFLY AND BERRY WATER SET

This was one of Fenton's most popular patterns. It was a pattern that seemed to adapt to almost any form. Shown here in cobalt blue, which is very desirable, it might easier be found in marigold, and for less money. In green you will find it much harder to come by, and in white it again is almost impossible to find. At this moment I don't recall seeing one in amethyst, though I am sure some were made, but they must have been on the minority side also. This set is another that many collectors have in two or more colors, if they can find them.

Crab Claw Water Set

Butterfly and Berry Water Set

DIAMOND AND THUMBPRINT WATER SET

Sometimes we walk over orchids while looking for roses. I never gave this water set much thought until it became apparent that it was one of the popular Millersburg patterns.

While researching the Millersburg story, we encountered bits and pieces of glass in this pattern and in all colors. These include white, amethyst, green, and even clear.

TIGER-LILY WATER SET

Shown here in marigold, which is not the most desirable color, but it is the one you are most likely to encounter. It came in amethyst and also in green and smoke. This is an Imperial Glass Company product. It was not made in ice blue in the beginning, but was reissued much later in ice blue, and does or should have an I.G. in the bottom. That is a capital G with a super-imposed I running through the letter G.

Diamond and Thumbprint Water Set

Tiger-Lily Water Set

FLORAL AND GRAPE WATER SET

This lovely water set, shown here in cobalt blue, may be found more easily in marigold and for somewhat less money. This must have been a big seller in marigold during the hey-day of Carnival. It seems like they made almost all of these in marigold and hardly any in cobalt blue, even though the cobalt blue was one of the Fenton favorites. Amethyst is not any more plentiful, and white is very scarce. Many people prefer the white, personally I like the cobalt blue. From the Neroni collection.

RASPBERRY WATER SET AND MILK PITCHER

There has been some confusion about this set. For reasons we can't explain, the water pitcher is smaller than most of the other pitchers — measuring about 8¾ inches high and about 3½ inches across the bottom. In many cases it has been mistaken for the milk pitcher, which measures about 7¼ inches high and almost the same size at the bottom as the water pitcher. For that reason we are showing the milk pitcher along with the water set. Almost all of them have the Northwood Mark, the N. in the bottom and may be found in marigold, amethyst, green and white, and if you are lucky, ice blue or ice green. Also there is a gravy boat that looks somewhat like a creamer, but I am sure it is not a creamer because to date there has been no sugar reported to match it.

Floral and Grape Water Set

Raspberry Milk Pitcher   Raspberry Water Set

HOB-STAR BAND WATER SET

Most collectors are not too well informed about this water set. Though it is a nice set, it apparently did not catch on too well when it was made. It looks very much like one of Imperial Glass Companies near-cut patterns. Also the flared bell-shaped tumbler points to Imperial. However this is not conclusive. It may well have come in all colors, though with the exception of one tumbler in emerald green, the only color we have seen is marigold. We have seen several tumblers in tumbler collections but the sets we have encountered are few.

ORANGE TREE VARIANT WATER SET

Fenton made at least four versions of the Orange Tree pattern. This one is sometimes referred to as the Orange Tree Orchard Variant and sometimes just as the Variant. Whichever you choose, I am quite sure people will know what you are referring to. I think this one is rather scarce for I have seen very few of these and what few I have seen were either blue or marigold, but I feel certain they were also made in green and white. This particular version of the Orange Tree pattern seems to have been used only on water sets.

SWIRL RIB WATER SET

This is a typical Northwood tankard pitcher and like most of the tankards, the N is missing. However, the tumblers usually have the N in the bottom. For some reason there are not too many of these around in any color. We have only seen these in marigold and green. Perhaps the lack of a more predominant pattern lessened the demand for this set. It is a good heavy glass and seems it would survive better than other sets that are in abundance.

Hob-Star Band Water Set

Orange Tree Variant Water Set

Swirl Rib Water Set

THE QUILL WATER SET

This Quill pattern is another one of the patterns carried over from the old pressed glass days. All indications are that this pattern was a lot more popular in the pressed glass days than in the heyday of the Carnival Glass, because we find very few of these. There are no marks to indicate the manufacturer, so we assume it was one of the smaller companies and not one of the Big Four. These are usually found in marigold and occasionally in amethyst. Other colors are quite possible.

JEWELED HEART WATER SET

Northwood used this pattern quite extensively as a secondary pattern on many bowls of various sizes and shapes. He even used this on some of the Farm Yard bowls and he used it on some of the peach-opalescent berry sets, so it is no wonder we find it on a water set. But why he used it so sparingly on the water sets makes us wonder. This set probably came in all colors but it usually is marigold — maybe one out of ten found in amethyst.

LEAF TIERS WATER SET

This was not one of the more popular patterns in Carnival Glass. The bowls must have been favored over the water sets, because we find berry sets and occasional bowls and table sets more readily than the water sets. I only recall seeing this water set in marigold and amethyst but I am sure there are some in blue and green. This set in any color is definitely scarce. It is probably Fenton's.

Quill Water Set

Jeweled Heart Water Set

Leaf Tiers Water Set

DIAMOND LACE WATER SET

This is another one of the Imperial Glass Company near-cut patterns that did so well in purple. Though this set is not that easy to find, even in purple, it is available. In marigold it is very difficult to find. I have only seen a couple of sets in the marigold, and only one tumbler in green, though I feel confident there were more made. How many survived, I don't know. I do know most any collector would enjoy having one in his collection.

FOUR SEVENTY FOUR WATER SET

This water set is scarce in any color. Shown here in marigold, the easiest one to find, followed closely by the green. The purple is almost impossible to find. This set was made by Imperial and this pattern was used on other pieces. It also has been reproduced but the new ones should be marked with an I.G.

BUTTERFLY AND FERN WATER SET

This set is one that is easy to identify. There are six of the large butterflies around the pitcher and the tumblers have three, and no guess-work about the fern leaves. This is such a gorgeous pattern one wonders why it was not used on other pieces as well as the water sets. Yet, it seems to have been confined to water sets and they were limited. Also limited to some extent on colors. Green must have been the favorite color, though there are some in amethyst and marigold, but very few. This is a Fenton product.

Diamond Lace
Water Set

Four Seventy Four
Water Set

Butterfly and Fern
Water Set

HEART AND FEATHER WATER SET

This is one of the more difficult sets to locate. May be found in marigold, amethyst or emerald-green. The iridescence and the shape of the pitcher lead us to believe it is Millersburg. From the Schleede collection.

GRAPE AND GOTHIC ARCHES WATER SET

The water set shown is rather scarce, and we find something different here. The pitcher has a faint N inside the circle; the tumblers have just the circle. Quite often on Northwood's water sets you will find the tumblers with the N, and the pitcher won't be marked at all. From the Schleede's collection.

PALM BEACH WATER SET

The Palm Beach pattern is really not too plentiful. Like many of the Grape patterns this is sometimes found on berry sets and four-piece table sets as well as water sets. These are found mostly in marigold and in white — you don't see many dark ones. This has been attributed to the United States Glass Company. There seems to be a difference in the color of their marigold — it is about halfway between an amber and marigold, at least some of them are. The white ones are usually a good frosty white.

Heart and Feather
Water Set

Grape and Gothic
Arches Water Set

Palm Beach
Water Set

NORTHWOOD PEACH WATER SET

Shown here in cobalt blue, which is the most difficult color to find in this pattern. It is also hard to find in marigold. For some reason, more of these were made, or at least survived, in white than in any other color. Yet a few years ago this same pattern could quite easily be found in clear, green, blue, and amethyst, often trimmed in gold, but not iridized of course. This being one of the old pressed glass patterns, perhaps Mr. Northwood felt this pattern was no longer desirable. Whatever the case may be, yesterday — today — this set is a treasure. Our thanks to Don and Connie Moore for the loan of this beautiful set.

IMPERIAL GRAPE WATER SET

Imperial Glass Company made tons of water sets and bowls in this pattern and of different colors, but few in the purple. A set in this color is a dream that won't come true for many people, there just are not enough of the purple to go around. Though these have been reproduced in other colors, I seriously doubt they will ever again equal the color and the iridescence we find on these purple sets. The new ones can be found easily in marigold and they are plainly marked with an I.G. This set also belongs to the Moore's.

BEADED SHELL WATER SET

This attractive water set was never made in great quantity, like many of the other Northwood patterns. This pattern was used on occasional bowls and four-piece table sets, as well as the mugs and berry sets. The marigold is the easier color to find in most cases except for the mug. The water sets are harder to locate in the dark and white, but this set is a find in any color.

Northwood Peach
Water Set

Imperial Grape
Water Set

Beaded Shell
Water Set

ROBIN WATER SET

Whether this particular pattern wasn't one of the favorites or whether kitchen sinks and careless hands took a heavy toll isn't clear. Nevertheless, this was the most difficult water set to find. It is far different than the Singing Birds which many mistake for the Robin. In all probability, it is the same basic pattern as the Robin mug. Apparently greater efforts were put forth in making the molds for the water set. The details are sharper and the pattern more striking. It is definitely Imperial.

This is a heavy, good quality glass and the iridescense is excellent. This water set is believed to be one of the very few that was made only in Marigold.

THE SINGING BIRDS WATER SET

This water set has almost disappeared from the open market. Very seldom do you find this at a show or in a shop. Most of these have found their way into collections. When collections go up for sale then you have a chance to get one. This is a Northwood pattern and most of the pieces are marked with the N on the bottom. This set came in all of the colors though not as many pastels as the marigold, purple and green. Equally desirable are the berry sets and four-piece table sets in this pattern.

WINDMILL WATER SET AND MILK PITCHER

This was one of Imperial Glass Company's popular water sets, because they made tons of them. Marigold was the favorite color by far, and today, they are far more plentiful than the green. The purple is almost impossible to find, which is usually reflected in the price. We are showing the milk pitcher with this set for comparison. The water set has been reproduced heavily, but we don't think the milk pitchers have been, though they could be before this gets into print. They are marked with the I.G. if they are reproduced — at least they are supposed to be, so they tell us.

Robin
Water Set

Singing Birds
Water Set

Windmill
Milk Pitcher

Windmill
Water Set

GRAPE AND CABLE WATER SET

The Grape and Cable was no doubt the most popular pattern ever used on Carnival Glass and the water sets got their share of the glory. As a rule, you find more marigold than amethyst in water sets but I think these are fairly evenly divided, especially with the regular size set. The amethyst is priced higher than the marigold, but the spread is not as great as it is on some of the others. The green in this pattern almost always is priced higher than the amethyst, because there are so few of them. These may also be found in the pastel colors, but are very scarce. This is Northwood's and most of them have the N in the bottom.

GRAPE AND CABLE TANKARD

We gave you a double-take on this one for comparison. Note the difference in the tumblers — they are larger — they are just a little higher and they flare out at the top, which makes them interesting. Many years ago I saw an ad in the Trader "Two Jumbo Grape and Cable Tumblers", and when they arrived, they were the tumblers for the tankard. The tankard sets are hard to find and priced much higher than the regular sets. These also came in all the colors and none of them are plentiful. I believe most of them carry the N mark, also.

ACORN BURR WATER SET

This massive pattern always stands out whether it's in a show, an auction or a collection at home. The pattern was never used to the extent of the Grape and Cable, but it was used on berry sets and four-piece table sets as well as punch bowls. It is Northwood and most have the N in the bottom and came in all the usual colors that Northwood made.

Grape and Cable
Water Set

Grape and Cable
Tankard

Acorn Burr
Water Set

FARMYARD BOWL

This one is definitely a collector's favorite, though there are several of these to be found. The price is still good. In the late fifties and early sixties this bowl was selling from $50.00 to $75.00. It soon climbed to a thousand and then on upwards. This was made by Northwood as one of the later patterns (1919-21). It is a masterpiece of color, iridescence, and workmanship. Just why he chose to omit the famous N is anybody's guess. Perhaps he knew it would be unmistakable because of the Jeweled Heart secondary pattern that no other company used. And this is one the reproductions have not hurt. The new ones are fairly easy to tell, as they don't have the color or the iridescence of the old ones.

PETER RABBIT BOWL

This is another version of Mr. Fenton's animal dishes and is a popular one too. Found in marigold most often, but several have shown up in blue and green. I don't recall any in amethyst or white. These may also be found in flat plates, and of course, the plates demand a substantial increase in price over the bowls. This has one of the characteristics of the Little Fishes bowl, the pattern just doesn't stand out too plainly and makes it hard to see. But at the prices it brings, I guess it really doesn't matter.

TEN MUMS LOW BOWL

Beyond a doubt, the designer of this pattern expected it to hang on a wall or be displayed on a buffet or shelf. The small wreath in the center rounds out the decorative effect and is placed perfectly to help determine the position of the bowl.

This piece still can be found in an occasional shop. I have not seen it mentioned in catalogs, even though I am certain that it was made by Fenton.

SECTION 3 — BOWLS

Farmyard Bowl

Peter Rabbit Bowl

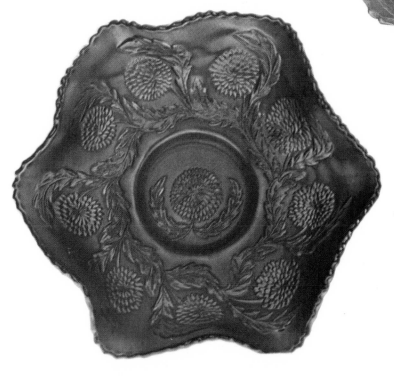

Ten Mums Low Bowl

DRAGON AND STRAWBERRY BOWL

This combination of the Dragon and Strawberry pattern is definitely on the scarce side. The strawberries are very well done, and fit gracefully into the space provided for them. I would personally choose the strawberries over the lotus, yet the Dragon and Lotus was made in abundance and the few of these around indicates a very small factory run. This is a Fenton product and may be found in marigold and blue. Other colors may have been made, but if so, we have not encountered them.

THE MILLERSBURG PEACOCK

Most glass companies have a version of the peacock. The Millersburg Glass Company was no exception.

Its version is perhaps the most sought. Collectors favor the fine detail and predominance of the bird. The urn has no beading and there is no bee, a feature of other Peacock and Urn patterns. In addition, the glass has splendid quality with exceptional iridescence.

PEACOCK AND GRAPE

Fenton Art Glass Company conceived this version of the peacock, combining two popular patterns into a pleasing presentation.

It was necessary to squeeze his tail just a mite in order to fit him into the panels and permit adequate display of the grape design.

The example shown is in azure blue.

Note: (inset) The bearded berry secondary pattern was used exclusively by Fenton.

Dragon and Strawberry Bowl

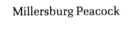

Millersburg Peacock

Peacock and Grape

FENTON'S THISTLE BANANA BOAT

Yes, Fenton had a try at the banana boat. It's smaller than the Grape and Cable and is becoming more popular. The exterior pattern is very familiar, Cat Tails and Water Lilies, and it is just as attractive in marigold.

NIPPON

Here is another Northwood design that seems simple, yet has a rare beauty. Strangely, it was produced in all the usual colors so one tends to pass it by, except for ice blue.

The major art glass collectors insist that this is not Carnival and they display it as Art Glass. This convinces me that I was right all along; Carnival glass belongs with the best.

Look for the (N).

PEACOCK AND URN — FENTON

This is similar to other peacock pieces but the bee is slightly larger and the urn has two rows of beads — top and bottom.

The bearded berry pattern decorates the reverse side. This, also, was made in the usual colors.

Fenton's Thistle Banana Boat

Nippon

Peacock and Urn
— Fenton

CORAL BOWL

This is one of the busy patterns that Fenton made and judging from the amount of them you see, was not one of the more popular ones. In many ways it is much like the Little Fishes bowl, and seems as though it was mostly confined to occasional bowls and not seen very often. I suspect many people wouldn't recognize it. It probably came in all colors but more often shows up in marigold, with a green now and then — usually has a modest price when offered for sale.

THE STAG AND HOLLY

This is believed to have been Fenton Art Glass Company's version of a fruit bowl for Christmas time.

The proud animals spaced with the holly leaves and exceptional berries together with the holly wreath in the center certainly suggest this motif.

The cobalt blue coloring is here mixed with the iridescence and tends to reproduce as green. This will be found in green, as well as marigold and, perhaps, purple.

THE PONY BOWL

Here is an animal pattern that Fenton did not make. We have the Greek Key pattern like Northwood made. Some feel that because of the shiny surface, it is Millersburg, which I seriously doubt, because we do find this Pony bowl in ice-green and ice-blue, which is another hint that this is Northwood's, as Northwood made almost all of the ice-blue and ice-green. This may also be found in amethyst. And I should add that this is another one that has recently been reproduced. However, a novice collector should be able to distinguish the difference.

Coral Bowl

Stag and Holly Bowl

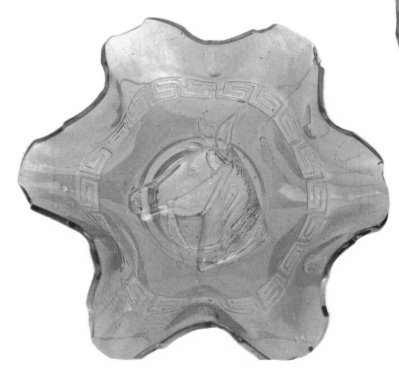

The Pony Bowl

STRAWBERRY (NORTHWOOD)

For the bowl collector this one is a must. This is a trifle smaller than the Strawberry you find with the berry sets and the strawberries are arranged a little differently from the Millersburg, which square off in the center of the bowl. This may or may not be marked with the N on the bottom of the bowl. This is usually found in amethyst, marigold or green but may also be found in the pastel colors as well.

FLOWERS AND WATER LILIES
or
FENTON'S TWO FLOWERS

Sometimes called Two Flower and sometimes called Flowers and Water Lilies, this large, footed fruit bowl made by the Fenton Art Glass Company is a distinguished pattern. This indeed is a beautiful piece, especially in cobalt blue.

THE PERSIAN GARDEN

In 1912 this coloring was called pearly edge; modern collectors refer to it as peach opalescent.

The pattern is not rare but it is in scarce supply. One cannot understand why Fenton would fail to produce an abundance of this artfully done design.

Perhaps the limited edition helped authenticate the "art glass" image that the manufacturer tried to create.

Strawberry (Northwood)
Bowl

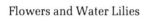

Flowers and Water Lilies

Persian Garden Bowl

THE BUTTERFLY AND TULIP

To find this piece requires more than a casual shopping tour.

Rarely does one find a single flower covering the entire surface of a bowl, this being the subject figure with the butterfly centered in proper perspective.

This is fine quality, heavy glass. The iridescence is excellent.

There are no identifying marks, the color is standard, and the pattern provides little help in determining the manufacturer.

THE DRAGON AND LOTUS LOW BOWL

The oriental pattern on this bowl helps to attract attention. But the exquisite red, with a touch of amberina around the base, marks it as an extremely rare item.

The amberina authenticates red glass as Carnival, a fact of which one should be aware when examining red pieces.

This is a product of Fenton Art Glass Company.

ROSE TREE BOWL

This is one of the more attractive patterns that Fenton made and is difficult to acquire. It is a shallow bowl about 3″ high and 10″ across at the widest point and has the Orange Tree pattern on the back side, which tells it was made by Fenton. Shown here in a beautiful cobalt blue, it no doubt came in all colors that Fenton normally made. There is always the possibility that they flattened one of these out for a chop plate. If so, I would assume it would be a dandy. This rare bowl is in the Moore's collection.

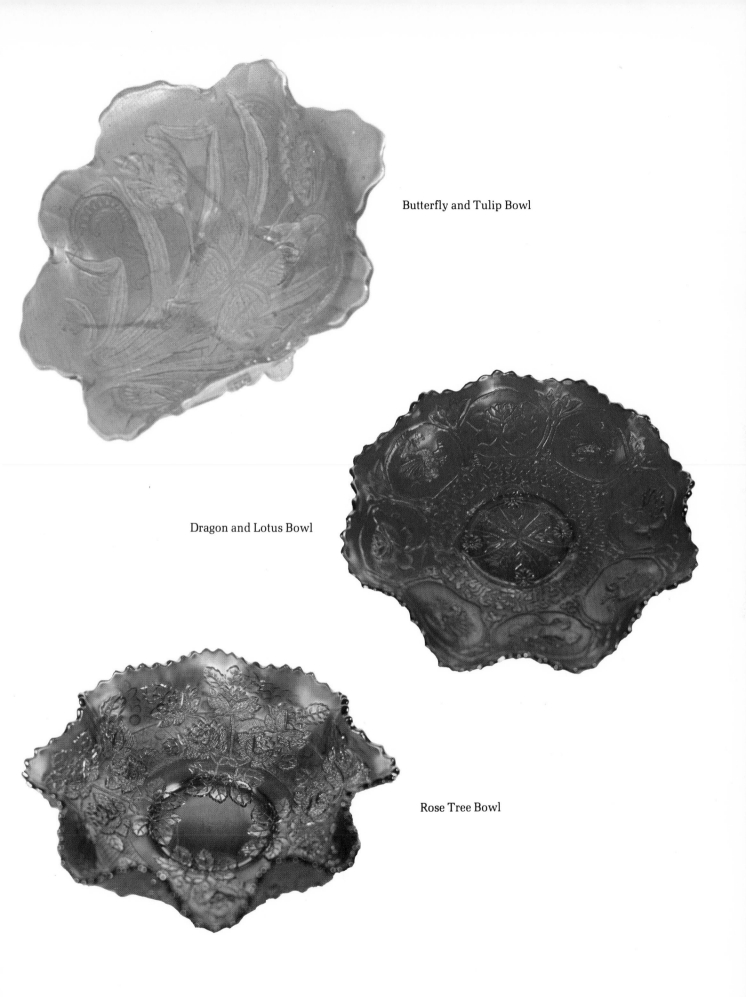

Butterfly and Tulip Bowl

Dragon and Lotus Bowl

Rose Tree Bowl

LUCKY BELL BOWL

We find the Horseshoe quite often on the Good-luck plates and bowls; we also find the Bell. But to find this combination in Carnival Glass is unique. I think this bowl is about 8½" across and about 4½" high. Probably it came in all the colors but this is the only one I have seen. Our thanks to the Pfaffs of North Carolina for this one.

THE NESTING SWAN

The combination of honey-amber coloring and the graceful swan surrounded by holly leaves and flowers commands attention in any collection. The fact that this is a Millersburg product has enhanced the demand.

This fruit bowl was made in numerous colors with honey amber and marigold leading in popularity.

THE BIG FISH (MILLERSBURG)

One wonders if the artist himself hooked that fish in Killbuck Creek near the Millersburg factory in Holmes County, Ohio.

Perhaps he merely dreamed of a catch like it.

It is evident that he did have an inspiration. The craftsmanship is magnificent, typical of the skills displayed throughout the Millersburg line.

This bowl is in amethyst. It can be found in green.

Lucky Bell Bowl

The Nesting Swan

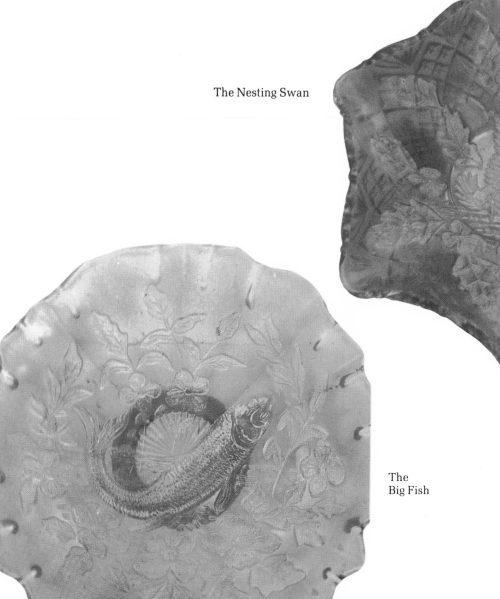

The
Big Fish

THE CAROLINA DOGWOOD

This Carolina Dogwood pattern is one that was carried over from the milk glass patterns and in this case, the components as well. Several companies made an opaque glass that was an off-white; someone dubbed it "milk glass" and the name stuck. Some people refer to it as Pearl Carnival. This looks almost like the peach-opalescent but if you look closely, there is a definite difference. There is very little of this around, which indicates a small run of this type of glass.

FENTON'S GOOD-LUCK BOWL

This piece is far different than the Good Luck bowl by Northwood that you are accustomed to seeing, and the supply is much more limited. Also the colors are limited. This is seldom, if ever, found in other than the marigold, shown here, however the Heart & Vine part of this pattern was used quite extensively on bowls and plates and advertising pieces. This lovely bowl is from the Moore's collection.

MILLERSBURG HOLLY WHIRL SAUCE BOAT

This looks like a creamer but since no other pieces were found to go with it, we believe it is a sauce dish. This opalescent was sold as iridescent art glass, so it probably was more decorative than anything else.

It was not made in great quantity as Millersburg Glass Company was in business only for about three years.

The Carolina Dogwood

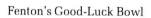

Fenton's Good-Luck Bowl

Holly Whirl Sauce Boat

THE FINE RIB BANANA DISH

This odd-shaped dish, believed to have been used as a banana dish, is a very simple, fine ribbed pattern with a ribbon candy edge. It is quite unique in peach opalescent.

This particular fine-rib was caused by the Northwood Glass Company but there were several that used a similar one. The exterior pattern looks very similar to the Caroline.

MILLERSBURG COURT HOUSE

There is no doubt as to the manufacturer of the Courthouse bowl. Most pieces have been found near the factory and likely were made to commemorate completion of the building. Apparently there was just one size bowl and some scalloped edges and some ruffles varied the design. It was a souvenir piece that was supposedly given to the stockholders, workers and residents of Millersburg. However, there really is not any way of checking that out. Some of the lettering was different, some are what are called "unlettered", some were lettered. The difference in lettering is at the base of the court-house. One interesting thing, the old courthouse today looks much like it did then.

BROOKLYN BRIDGE

This is also a souvenir bowl, but we don't know who made it. Many people think Northwood, some think Millersburg. I don't think either one made them, or else we would have found them in other colors. It seems more likely that some small company put them out, but that is of little significance. It is a desirable piece and highly collectable. They seem to be all one size, one shape, one color — and that color is marigold, as shown here. It is possible other colors and shapes were made, but if so we have not found them.

Fine Rib Banana Dish

Millersburg Court House

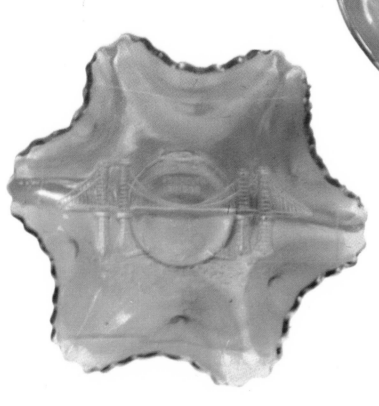

Brooklyn Bridge

GRAPE AND CABLE ORANGE BOWL

This large, footed fruit bowl is believed to have been designed for Christmas holiday festivities.

It brings back pleasant memories, primarily of such a bowl as this heaped with pop corn balls.

This is a Northwood product. The (N) is inscribed inside on the bottom.

ICE BLUE GRAPE AND CABLE CENTERPIECE BOWL

The Grape and Cable centerpiece bowl is almost as desirable as the Grape and Cable Fernery. Shown here in ice-blue, which is probably the favorite color, though the ice-green is equally as hard to find. In fact, there is no abundant supply of these in any color. In the old catalogs we find one of these advertised as a salad bowl, with the points turned up instead of turning in like they normally do, but they are also on the scarce side. This same bowl design is shown elsewhere in the book with the matching candlesticks and in a different color. After all, it's the colors of Carnival that are fascinating. Most of these have the N in the bottom.

THE CHERRY WREATH

This oval fruit bowl, or berry dish, is similar to the banana boats and was sold with six sauce dishes as a set.

Some collectors claim that it was made by the Diamond Glass Company, inasmuch as they have found butter dish bases with a "D" inside a diamond.

However, there is no record as evidence that Diamond ever made Carnival Glass. We know that Harry Northwood was associated with Diamond and later purchased it. Perhaps he obtained molds from them. Certainly, the pattern has distinct Northwood characteristics.

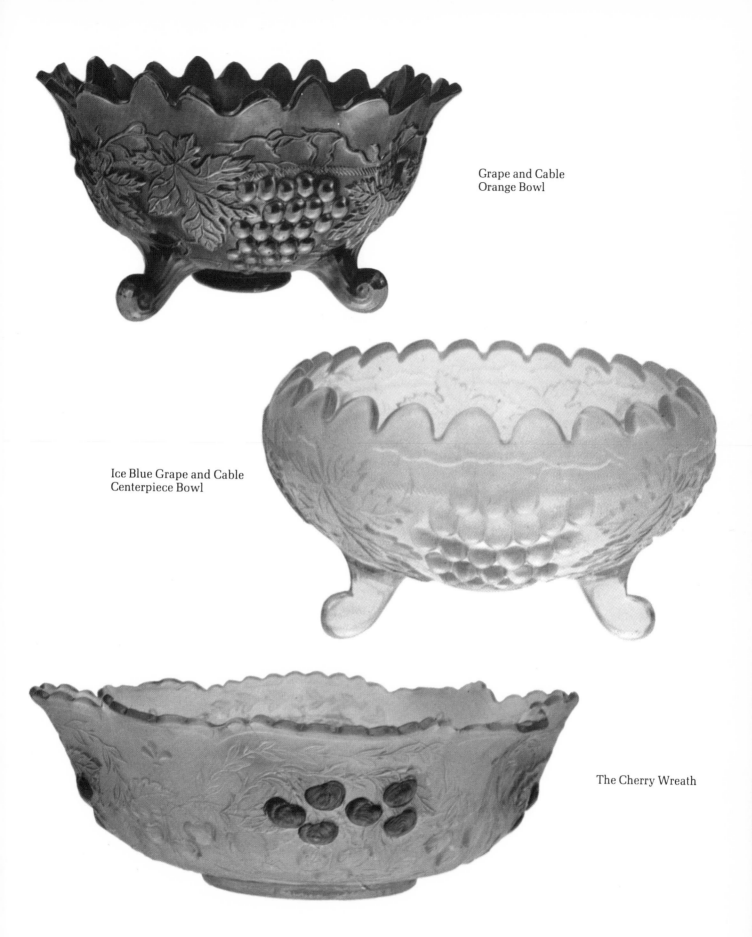

Grape and Cable
Orange Bowl

Ice Blue Grape and Cable
Centerpiece Bowl

The Cherry Wreath

77

PEACOCK AT THE FOUNTAIN ORANGE BOWL

This Orange Bowl is somewhat smaller than the Grape & Cable Orange Bowl but was probably used much the same way — as a catch-all. This usually was not sought after as much as the Grape & Cable until one was found in aqua-opalescent, which sold at an auction for over the two thousand dollar mark. This is Northwood's and usually has the (N) marking. It came in all the normal colors that Northwood made.

STRAWBERRY (MILLERSBURG)

This low bowl is a collector's item, for sure, as are any of the Millersburg pieces. The entire pattern is very graceful with fine stippling on the leaves and prominent berries. The veins in the leaves are outstanding craftsmanship, typical of the Millersburg Glass Company.

The color is amethyst with the fine iridescence that sets Millersburg apart.

FENTON'S GRAPE AND CABLE

This salad bowl may be mistaken for the centerpiece bowl.

However, the points go upwards, the leaves are different, the (N) is missing and the color varies. It is attractive enough to be a popular collector's item but has not appeared frequently. It probably was made in all colors although I have seen only marigold and blue.

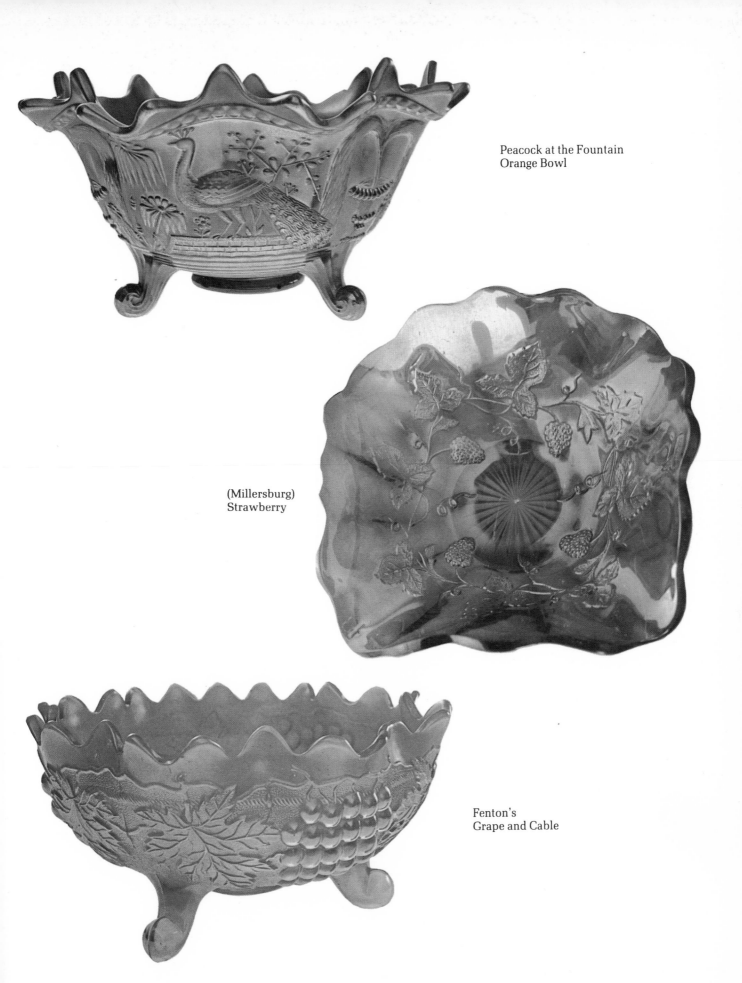

Peacock at the Fountain
Orange Bowl

(Millersburg)
Strawberry

Fenton's
Grape and Cable

LOTUS AND POINSETTIA

This is a variation of the Dragon and Lotus except the Poinsettia replaces the Dragon. Note that the Lotus forms a cross like the dogwood blossom, which makes it an interesting specimen. This is a large footed fruit bowl 10″ across and 3¼″ high. It probably came in all colors and is shown here in a typical Fenton cobalt blue.

LATTICE AND POINSETTIA

This is another one of the graceful patterns by Northwood and seldom marked with the N. It came in two different shaped bowls. Some are footed with three feet, some have just a plain collar base. The sizes vary depending on how much they flared out, and once in a lifetime you might find one that was flattened out into a plate. We saw one in azure blue, the color shown here, and it was very striking, but not for sale.

DOUBLE STEM ROSES

This is unusual because we find so little pastel green and blue made by Fenton Art Glass Company. Most glass in these hues came from Northwood.

Despite the ribbon candy edge that appeared on the Farm Yard, this is decidedly Fenton.

Lotus and Poinsettia

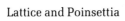

Lattice and Poinsettia

Double Stem Roses

SMOOTH RAYS FRUIT BOWL

In this bowl, the base glass is an over-balanced amethyst which many have described as red.

The inside pattern is a simple, smooth ray design with no stippling of any kind. The exterior pattern is the Beaded Heart, sometimes called Jewel Heart, an exclusive Northwood design. It appears on the Farm Yard Bowl.

The color and iridescence on this bowl will rival the best, even the Farm Yard.

FENTON'S WINDMILL AND MUMS

This is far different than Imperial's windmill. The water scene, sail boats, coast line with buildings and the evenly spaced mums comprise a display piece. I doubt if anyone could find the heart to put fruit or anything else in it.

The dimensions are 10½ inches across and 4½ inches high. The glass and iridescence are excellent.

LITTLE FISHES BOWL

Although these are not as large as the Millersburg Big Fish, they are as well executed and the grass and rushes are extremely artistic.

It is an attractive design that required many hours to produce. I would guess that Mr. Fenton crafted this pattern himself, inasmuch as he was responsible for several of the finer Fenton Art Glass designs.

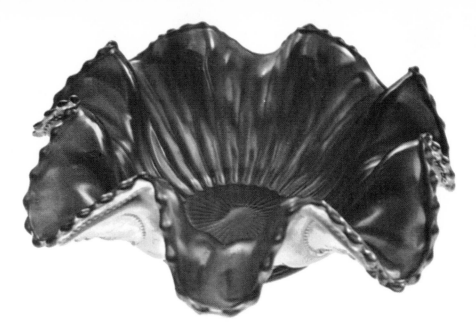

Smooth Rays
Fruit Bowl

Fenton's Windmill and
Mums

Little Fishes Bowl

COSMOS — VARIANT

This piece proves that the artists of 50 years ago were also master craftsmen.

The fashioning of a graceful design such as this from a single blossom and a wreath of leaves is a worthy achievement.

There are no identifying marks or secondary patterns to give a hint as to the manufacturer but the amethyst color and fine iridescence point to Millersburg.

THE VICTORIAN

This large fruit bowl is not common. It is thought to have been especially made as a bride's basket, although I have seen only one in a frame.

The glass quality is splendid, the iridescence exceptional. The manufacturer has not been determined.

RAYS AND RIBBONS

This lovely Millersburg pattern duplicates designs by Imperial and Northwood.

The fancy ribbon around the outside and the addition of the Hob Star and Feather design on the exterior distinguishes this one from the others.

I found several broken pieces of the Hob Star pattern in Millersburg. Some call it the Hob Star and Fern.

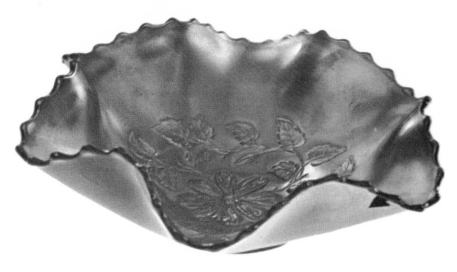

Cosmos Variant

Victorian

Rays and Ribbon

CHERRY BOWL (NORTHWOOD)

Probably, this fruit bowl seldom had much fruit in it. More than likely, Grandma kept it tucked in the china closet and put it into use only on the most special occasions.

The Beaded Heart exterior designates it as Northwood although the (N) is absent.

GRAPE AND CABLE ICE-CREAM BOWL

These ice-cream sets were very popular when they were made. At that time you did not run down to the corner and buy a quart or half-gallon of ice-cream. People had their own home freezers and made their own ice-cream. Most of the freezers were the gallon type — a can set in a wooden bucket. They put ice and rock salt around it and turned the hand crank until the cream froze, then they would dip it out into this large bowl. There were six smaller dishes that went with this large bowl for individual servings. This came in all the colors, made by Northwood, and most have the N in the bottom.

STIPPLED PETAL FRUIT BOWL

This very simple pattern of petals arranged somewhat differently than they would naturally grow, with a little stippling, created a very pleasing arrangement. This was just an occasional bowl, or catch-all, but the peach-opalescent coloring makes up for anything that might be missing. One look at the bowl will tell us why this was advertised as "iridescent art glass". Though there are no marks, we feel confident this is Northwood.

Cherry Bowl
(Northwood)

Grape and Cable
Ice Cream Bowl

Stippled Petal
Fruit Bowl

RAIN DROPS BOWL

This pleasing pattern seems to be another that was used almost exclusively for small fruit bowls, and peach-opalescent in color. The sizes vary on this one depending on how much it is flared and the edges crimped. The simple little raindrops pattern makes a delightful design, especially for the peach color. This may have come in other colors; if so, very few survived. This is also a Northwood product.

CHERRY CIRCLES
(Fenton's Cherries)

This large bowl is so low it could be used as a sandwich plate or a fruit bowl. The one shown here is 10½″ across and 2″ high. Some are flatter than this one and a little wider across the top. The pattern seems to be limited to this particular type bowl, and I believe it came in all the usual colors that Fenton made except red, for none of these have been reported in red. Who knows, one may show up yet!

FEATHER STITCH

I am not quite sure where this pattern got its name. They tell me that women use an embroidery stitch with this name. It almost reminds me of small mesh chicken-wire. Whatever the artist had in mind, it is quite nice. But somehow this pattern did not catch on and for some reason, you don't encounter many of these. This is believed to be Fenton.

Rain Drops Bowl

Cherry Circles

Feather Stitch

TREE OF LIFE AND FAN

Iridescent art glass was the appropriate name for this piece. We now refer to it as Peach Opalescent. We have not seen any reissues of this. We think it was made by Northwood, although there is no mark. They did make the Tree of Life pattern and also the Fan pattern.

THE SKI STAR FRUIT BOWL

I'm not sure where the name Ski Star originated but it is a lovely pattern. This is another pattern especially designed for Peach Opalescent. I don't recall seeing it in any other colors. It seems to be a little on the scarce side now. It is a Fenton product.

PEACH AND PEAR OVAL BOWL

Although it is often referred to as a Banana Boat, we don't class these with Banana Boats because they are not footed. They sit on a base. We have seen this in an oval frame like a bride's basket. I would like to point out quickly I never authenticated them as such. Until I have more information I will still classify them as Oval Bowls. They were apparently made in different colors. We don't know the manufacturer.

Tree of Life
and Fan Bowl

The Ski Star
Fruit Bowl

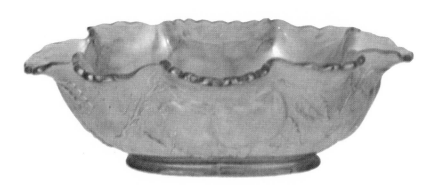

Peach and Pear
Oval Bowl

FLEUR DE LIS

I can only speculate that geography figured in the creation of this design.

The Millersburg Glass Company, as you know, imported workers from Europe. Since this is a national symbol in France, little is left except to guess the circumstances.

Millersburg did make beautiful art glass and Mr. Fortune found scrap examples of this pattern near the factory site. This piece is amethyst. The iridescence is exceptional.

PEACOCK AND GRAPE — RED BOWL

We have two very popular patterns combined on this bowl. This came in all the usual colors but red is the chosen color for this one. Occasionally you will find a flat plate in this pattern but the plates are extremely rare, and a red in this pattern would be high. This is a Fenton piece.

ELK BOWL

Commemorative bowls may have at one time been an inducement for membership. If not then, it surely would be today. These were made in plates as well as bowls, though I think they used the mould and just flattened them out into plates while they were still hot. There also is a bell and a paperweight, but the paperweight, we think, was made by Millersburg, while this version of the bowl was made by Fenton. These came mostly in blue, though some may be found in amethyst or green. I don't recall seeing one in marigold.

Fleur De Lis

Peacock and Grape
Red Bowl

Elk Bowl

SHELL AND SAND

Shell and Sand pattern is most often found on fruit bowls. It probably was not one of the more popular patterns at the peak of Carnival, but it is attractive shown here in a light green. Again the marigold is my favorite. This piece has been credited to Imperial because it was shown grouped with Imperial pieces in some of the trade catalogs, but I still wonder if it didn't come from Westmoreland.

SINGLE FLOWER FRAMED

It is a shame that the manufacturer did not mark pieces like this so we could pay them the tribute they rightfully have coming. This is one of the few pieces that will rival the Farm Yard Bowl at its finest for color and iridescence. The small scale-effect stippling leads us to suspect Fenton, but without more information we can't be certain.

ORANGE TREE CENTERPIECE BOWL

This one we believe truly belongs in the class with the centerpiece bowls. It probably was flattened out from the Orange bowl and is large, measuring 12″ wide and about 4″ high. When held to the light it is a deep cobalt blue but the lovely iridescence shows much purple and green. It was made by Fenton, and is in the collection of the Moores.

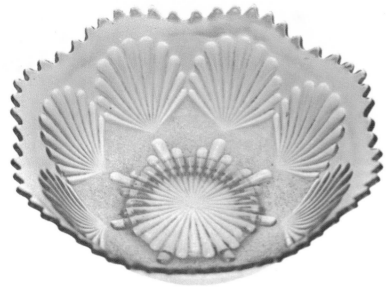

Shell and Sand

Single Flower Framed

Orange Tree
Centerpiece Bowl

SUNFLOWER

This is about the only pattern of a flower large enough to cover the whole bowl. Of course the sunflower is sometimes that big. This comes in different colors, but green seems to dominate the field. The underside of this carries one of Northwood's secondary patterns, so we think it is a Northwood piece.

DOGWOOD SPRAY

This puts us back in the art glass field again. Most of the peach opalescent Carnival Glass was made by only two companies, Northwood and Fenton. This particular one we think is Northwood despite the fact that there is no (N). This bowl measures 9 inches across and 3½ inches high.

COSMOS AND CANE

This pattern is found mostly on bowls, occasionally a water set, and almost every time in white. This leads us to believe it was made by some smaller company that primarily made crystal. However, it is attractive and highly collectible.

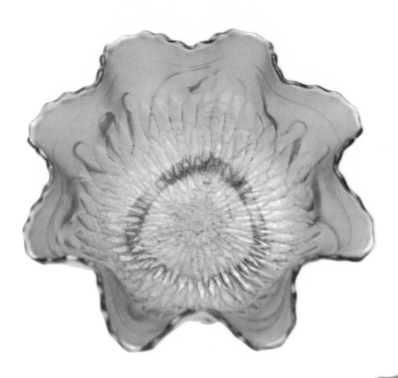

Sunflower

Dogwood Spray

Cosmos and Cane

CARNIVAL THISTLE

This is quite different from Fenton's Thistle Banana boat, shown elsewhere in the book, and different from the Inverted Thistle. It can also be found in green, marigold and blue as well as amethyst as shown here. This is made by Fenton.

GRAPE LEAVES AND ACORNS

It would be hard to guess just what the artist had in mind when he designed this pattern. I can't recall anything just like this in Leaves and Acorns. Nevertheless, it is quite pleasing. Maybe we just have to use our imagination. Sometimes it is very difficult to distinguish between Millersburg and Fenton pieces, but we think this is Fenton.

MILLERSBURG VINTAGE

At first glance this could be mistaken for the Millersburg Grape, but a second glance will tell you there is a difference. Instead of three bunches of grapes there are five. Note the tendrils. Instead of the Hobnail pattern on the underside we have the Wide Panel, or Optic if you wish. This may also be found in green and amethyst.

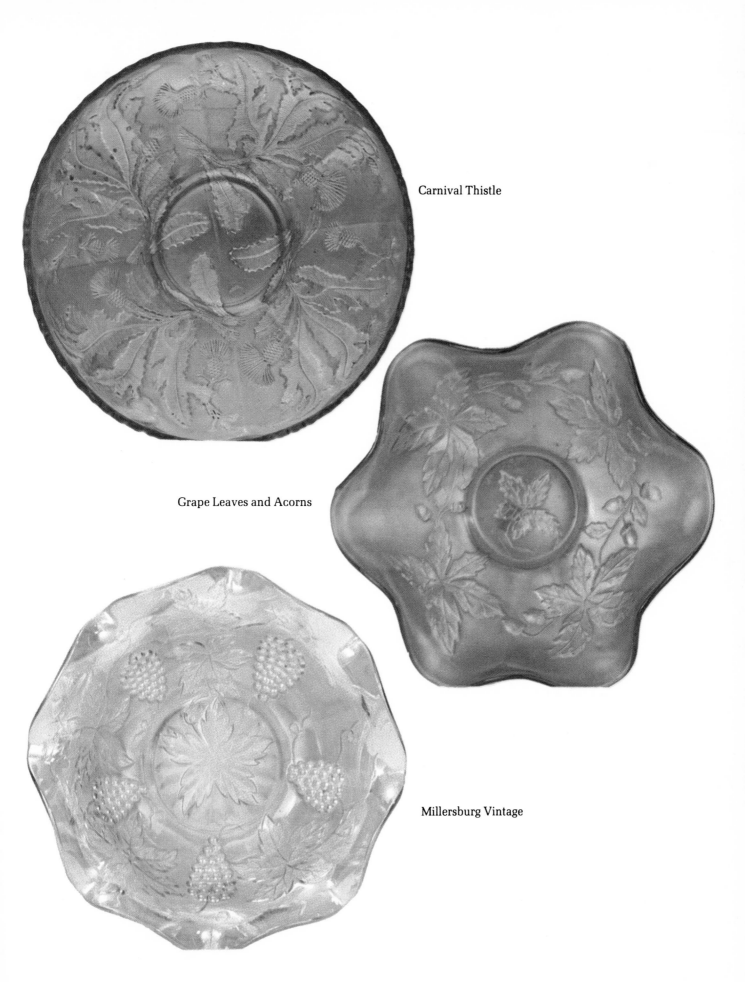

Carnival Thistle

Grape Leaves and Acorns

Millersburg Vintage

MANY STARS

A more suitable name would be most difficult to find for this bowl with a big star in the center, then more stars. Maybe that is why it is so attractive. This is another pattern we authenticated from pieces dug at the old Millersburg plant. We have seen this only in bowls and only in two colors, amethyst and green. No doubt there were others.

HOLLY AND BERRIES

We try to show good pieces of red. We can never get across the point too strongly that if it is not a good cherry red, it is not Red Carnival Glass. Many people have bought a slightly over-balanced amethyst for Red Carnival. This piece was made by Fenton.

GRAPE AND LOTUS LOW BOWL

In many ways this is different from the Dragon and Lotus, yet we have the same flower arranged somewhat the same. We have a different type of leaf which I would hardly classify as grape. Perhaps it best created the effect the artist had in mind. This is a Fenton product and scarce.

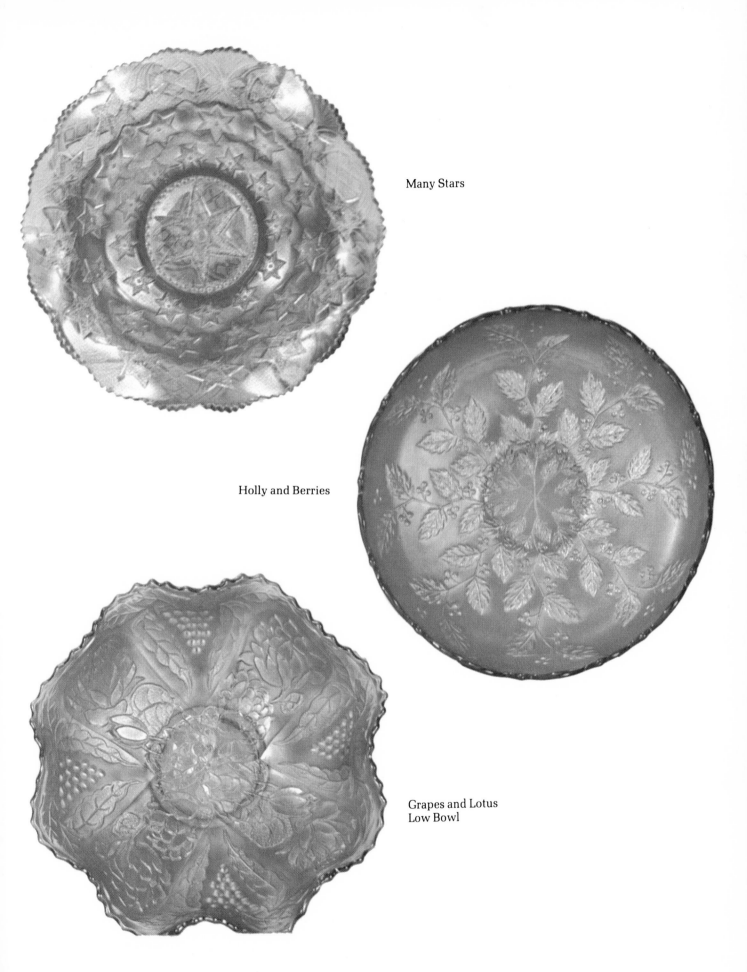

Many Stars

Holly and Berries

Grapes and Lotus
Low Bowl

FEATHERED SERPENT

Here is another nice one that doesn't fall in the rare category, yet is nice enough to grace most any collection. It may be found in berry sets though usually in an average size ruffled bowl about 10 inches wide by about 3 inches high. We think this was made at Millersburg and later at Fenton's factory.

COIN DOT

This is another pleasing pattern that can be found in different colors though not so many shapes. Look mostly for bowls about 9 inches wide by about 4 inches high. Some may or may not have the Ribbon Candy edge. This is thought to be a Fenton product but other companies may have made similar items.

ZIG ZAG

This is a pattern that puzzled collectors for years, including myself until we went to the site of the old Millersburg glass plant. After digging up pieces of glass with this pattern in green, marigold, and amethyst, we knew for sure it was made by Millersburg. So far we have only been able to find this pattern on bowls, but it is highly possible it was made in other pieces also.

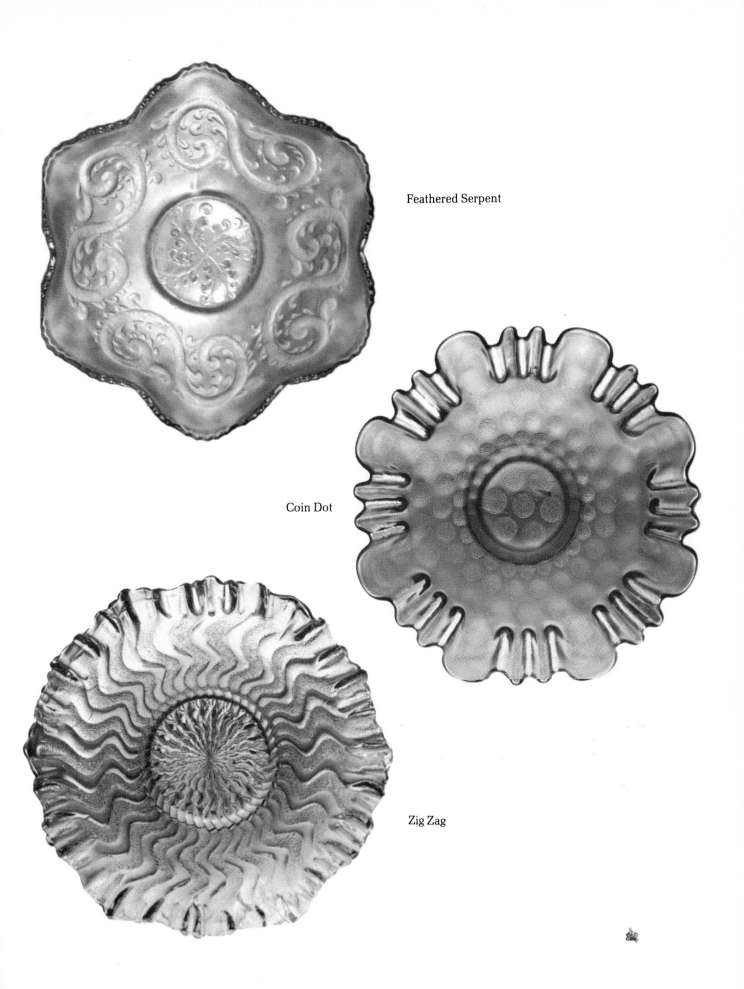

Feathered Serpent

Coin Dot

Zig Zag

PINE CONE BOWL

This little bowl is so attractive you would like to find five more and the large bowl to fill out the berry set, but experience has led us to believe there never was a large bowl. It looks like a sauce dish like many other sets have, but if there is a large one, it has been very elusive. We think it was just a small candy dish. Some were flattened out for a small plate, but they are in the minority. These were thought to have been made by Fenton, but we have no way to authenticate it.

SEA WEED LOW BOWL

This is another Millersburg piece with that little dot in the center that some people refer to as the Jeweler's Bead, be this fact or fiction. I personally have found this mark only on certain pieces of Millersburg glass. Every piece I have found with this mark has been of exceptional quality glass and fine iridescence. I have seen this pattern only on low bowls. Also we have seen it only in amethyst, marigold, and green.

AUTUMN ACORNS BOWL

Seldom do you find a pattern more easy to identify that this one. This small bowl measures only 7½" across by 2¼ high. It is very attractive and usually has good color — most often in marigold or blue, but on occasion may be found in green. You may be lucky to find one in red, for they are scarce and the price is usually much more. As Fenton made the bulk of red, we assume this is Fenton.

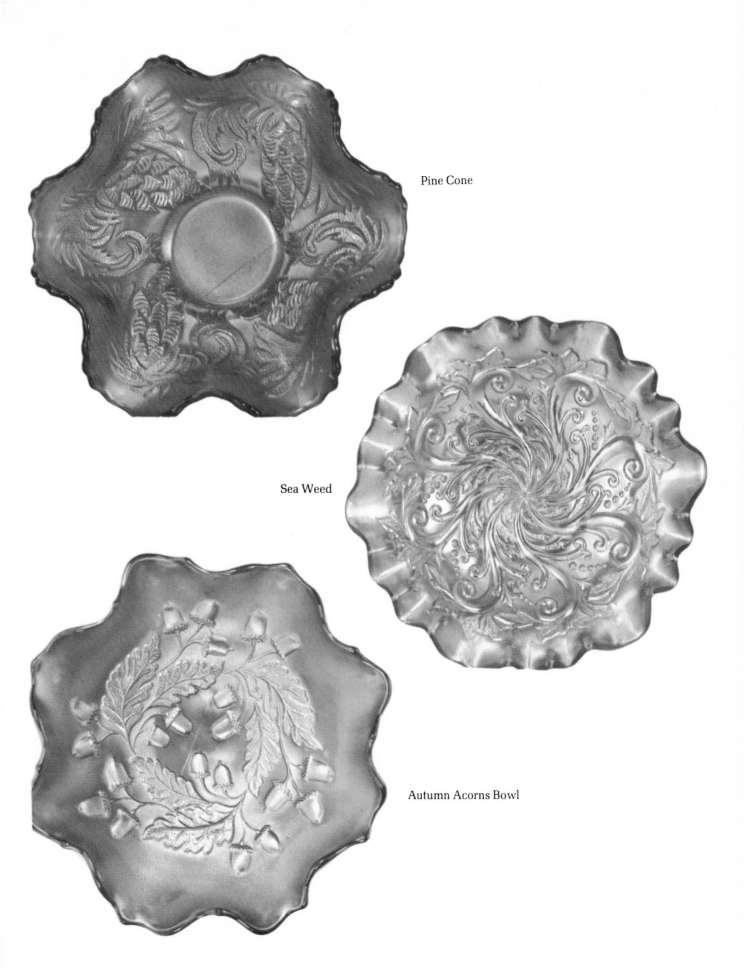

Pine Cone

Sea Weed

Autumn Acorns Bowl

THE KITTEN'S DISH

Some people refer to this as a saucer. Rather than get into any controversy, I will just say dish. I will say it is highly collectible and scarce. Even the small pieces bring good money. This was made by Fenton.

PRIMROSE

I doubt if I would need to tell you the name of this pattern. It is so well done you would be almost sure to guess. This is a typical Millersburg green. It is very attractive in amethyst and may also be found in marigold. We have never seen this pattern on any pieces except small bowls, although there may be others.

PODS AND POSIES

Occasionally you will still find this one in a shop at a fairly modest price. It also comes in a variety of colors. This seems to be about the size and shape of the average, but every so often you will find a plate. The flat plate in this is a find.

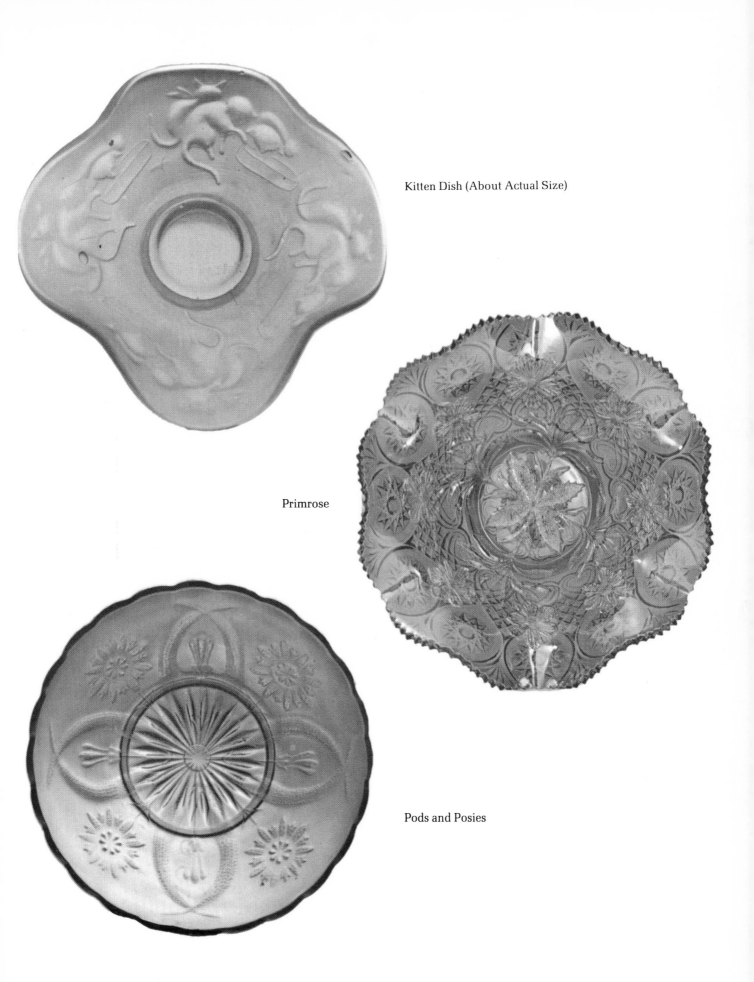

Kitten Dish (About Actual Size)

Primrose

Pods and Posies

HEART AND VINE

This is a nice one made by Fenton. Mr. Fenton must have been proud of this pattern because he used it often on advertising pieces, especially plates. It apparently wasn't too adaptable to other pieces such as water sets.

MORNING GLORY AND DRAPE

One of the nice peach opalescent pieces; it would be difficult to identify the maker. There are possibly some small sauce dishes to go with this, however, we have never seen any. Thanks to the Sam Wolfe's.

FANCY FLOWERS COMPOTE

A very attractive compote. Though not as large as some of the open compotes, this near-cut pattern produces a very pleasing effect. Many people think it is Millersburg, but I would hesitate to assign it to any particular manufacturer.

HEARTS AND FLOWERS VARIANT

This is somewhat different from the Hearts and Flowers by Northwood that we find quite often in ice-blue. Nonetheless it is attractive and would grace most any collection. It is unmarked.

Morning Glory and Drape

Heart and Vine

Fancy Flowers Compote

Hearts and Flowers
Variant

NORTHWOOD PEACH
Four-Piece Table Setting

One of the oldest patterns in Carnival, the Peach, appeared in 1906 in white and later in clear and green.

I haven't seen any catalogues showing this pattern. However, the Northwood Grape and some other well-known patterns were advertised widely by 1910 so it is highly possible that Northwood used the Peach pattern to start his famous iridescent line. This is the predominant reason for the desirability of this pattern.

Note on the (N)

Harry Northwood used a double circle surrounding his initial on pieces made prior to 1910. The center section was raised.

He simplified the design after that date, as shown.

PEACOCK AT THE FOUNTAIN
Four-Piece Table Setting

This popular version of the Peacock was made by Northwood.

It is not as scarce as the Millersburg Peacock, yet it commands attention wherever it is shown. Perhaps the large size of the butter dish and the well-displayed figure account for the popularity.

The spooner is often mistaken for an open sugar. It was customary to leave the set in the center of the dining table and the spooner held the family's every-day spoons. Modern kitchens made the spooner obsolete.

Apparently, this pattern can be found in a variety of colors.

CHERRY AND THUMBPRINT TABLE SET

This is another of Northwood's productions. We think the artist did an exceptionally fine job on this one. It came as a four-piece set. The creamer is missing as you can see. This set came in all the usual colors, and I think all the pieces are marked with the (N).

SECTION 4

Northwood Peach

Peacock at the Fountain

Cherry and Thumbprint
Table Set

THE NORTHWOOD GRAPE AND CABLE
Dresser Set

Beyond any doubt, this is a rare set, especially in marigold. It is one of few that is more plentiful in purple or green.

The perfume bottle is most difficult to locate, possibly because sets were sold with or without this item. The listing from the Baltimore Bargain Book of 1912 (inset) offers the set without it. I have seen no listings that include it.

The book listing establishes the date of first manufacture of this set. Evidently the perfume bottle was added later.

IRIDESCENT GLASS BUREAU SET.

New this season. Colors won't wash off.

★A2132—Set consists of 2 cologne bottles, height 9 inches; 1 hat pin holder, height 7 in.; 1 covered puff box, height 3½ inches; 1 pin tray, 5¾ inches; 1 comb and brush tray, 11¼ inches; raised grape pattern; 3 colors equally assorted, wine ruby, Nile green and golden iridescent glass; each set packed in partitioned cardboard box.......doz. sets, **$9.00**
Less than doz. sets.................set. **80c**

THE GRAPE AND CABLE WHISKEY SET

This whiskey decanter equals some of Northwood's finest work. A highly collectible, extra heavy, rare piece, it is valuable with or without the shot glasses.

The decanter illustrated has a solid glass stopper. Some produced with hollow-mushroom stoppers.

The tumblers, or shot glasses, represent a different tradition in whiskey consumption. They are larger than today's "jigger" by about one and one-half times. The dimensions are: 2¾ inches high, 2¼ inches wide at the top, 1¾ inches wide at the bottom.

This set was made in purple and marigold. Again, the marigold is more difficult to acquire.

Grape and Cable
Dresser Set

Grape and Cable
Whiskey Set

GRAPE AND CABLE CENTERPIECE SET

This giant bowl looks like a rose bowl. It was made especially for a center piece with a pair of matching candlesticks although it will not always be found like this.

It was often used as a "catch-all." Perhaps that is why we have so much trouble finding the candle sticks today. They undoubtedly were broken while being shifted around. I doubt if any of these things were deliberately destroyed for they were cherished then as much as today.

The sets came in a variety of colors and the bowls almost always carry the (N) mark. The candle sticks might or might not be marked, but you would be certain to recognize them as Northwood.

THE GOLDEN HARVEST WINE DECANTER

The name of this pattern, which combines grapes and a shock of wheat, is particularly appropriate.

Unlike some other decanters, the stopper on this one is solid glass, instead of the hollow mushroom stopper.

This has six Vintage wine glasses that are quite different from the Imperial Grape wine. The stem and foot are clear and plain. Four mold marks are visible. Why the decanter pattern is not duplicated on the glasses we do not know, but we are told this is the proper wine glass for this decanter set.

Having seen no others, we are inclined to believe that these are the proper ones. This set was made by the United States Glass Company.

Grape and Cable Center Piece

Golden Harvest Wine Decanter

NORTHWOOD'S PEACOCK AND URN ICE CREAM SET

This was one of the popular Ice Cream sets — the large bowl and six matching small bowls. Though we show only two of the small bowls, I assure you there were four more. Note — this urn has three rows of beads. The set came in all the normal colors that Northwood made, including aqua-opalescent, and most of the pieces are marked with the famous N on the bottom.

PEACOCK AT THE FOUNTAIN BERRY SET

Because of so many inquiries about this set, we are including it here. Note the small dishes do not have the peacock, just the flowers and the little sprigs or leaves. Only the big bowl has the peacock. The small dishes have the (N) as well as the large bowl. This set comes in all the usual colors. The ice blue shown here is usually the most difficult to find. This was made by Northwood.

Northwood's Peacock and Urn Ice Cream Set

Peacock at the Fountain Berry Set

GRAPE AND CABLE

This breakfast set is quite different from the creamer and sugar that come with the Grape and Cable four-piece table set. They are smaller and the sugar is an open sugar, whereas in the four-piece set, the sugar has a cover. Most of these have the N in the bottom and apparently came in all colors, though more often are found in purple or marigold and an occasional white.

LITTLE ORANGE TREE

Again, the Little Orange Tree breakfast set is quite different from the regular four-piece table set. The pieces are smaller and the sugar had no cover. These little fellows must not have been too popular, because they are hard to find. You find the four-piece table set fairly easily, but the breakfast set is difficult to find. Possibly it came in all the colors, but this one in cobalt blue is the only set we have encountered, though I am sure more were made. This is from Fenton.

SHELL AND JEWEL

The Shell and Jewel pattern is one that Westmoreland carried over from the old pressed glass days. This is also just a breakfast set. The sugar and creamer were all that came with this set, and there was no four-piece table set in this pattern. Why we don't know, as they used this pattern quite extensively in the pressed glass, but apparently not in Carnival glass. Both pieces had covers; the covers were not iridized on the green sets, but were on the marigold sets.

STRUTTING PEACOCK

The Strutting Peacock creamer and sugar was a breakfast set and the only pieces Westmoreland used this pattern for, at least in Carnival glass. Again, both pieces had covers, but the covers were not iridized. These were reproduced, but they are all supposed to be marked with a "W" running through a letter "G" for Westmoreland Glass Company. Also, the covers on the new ones are iridized, while on the old ones they were not.

ESTATE CREAMER AND SUGAR

This is a souvenir piece from Alexandria Bay, N.Y., the Heart of the Thousand Islands, a very popular resort center where Lake Ontario flows into the mighty St. Lawrence River. Thousands of tourists go there every year, so it is not surprising to find souvenir pieces. I was surprised to find one in Carnival Glass. Again we think this was commercial and it is difficult to trace the manufacturer.

Grape and Cable

Little Orange Tree

Shell and Jewel

Strutting Peacock

Estate Creamer and Sugar

THREE FRUITS AND FLOWERS FOOTED BON BON

At first glance this seems to be simply Three Fruits. However, the tiny flowers set it apart.

I show this because of the aqua coloring with the trace of white opalescence on the edge and a bit of brown or butterscotch down the side. This piece nearly always has the (N).

BUTTERFLY BON BON

I have passed many advertising pieces by not examining the under side. There often is no indication on top that a name, in this case Horlacher, is inscribed on the collar. Horlacher made chocolate candy.

This is probably a Fenton product, although I wouldn't rule out Millersburg because of amethyst coloring and shiny iridescence.

THE FOOTED BANANA DISH

Rarely do we find Carnival Glass bowls with metal feet. Some doubt arises that this is a factory feature but a silver plated foot in this case is a necessity.

The bowl does not have the (N) but the basket weave and the cool ice green identify the maker as Northwood.

BASKET WEAVE VARIANT ICE BLUE BON BON

This basket weave is different from the familiar basket weave you find marked with the (N). However we still think this was made by Northwood. It is a lovely piece and highly collectible.

BLACK BERRY MINIATURE COMPOTE

This little fellow is very charming and we suggest more decorative than anything else. It is shown here in cobalt blue and may also be found in marigold. These we feel reasonably sure were made by Fenton.

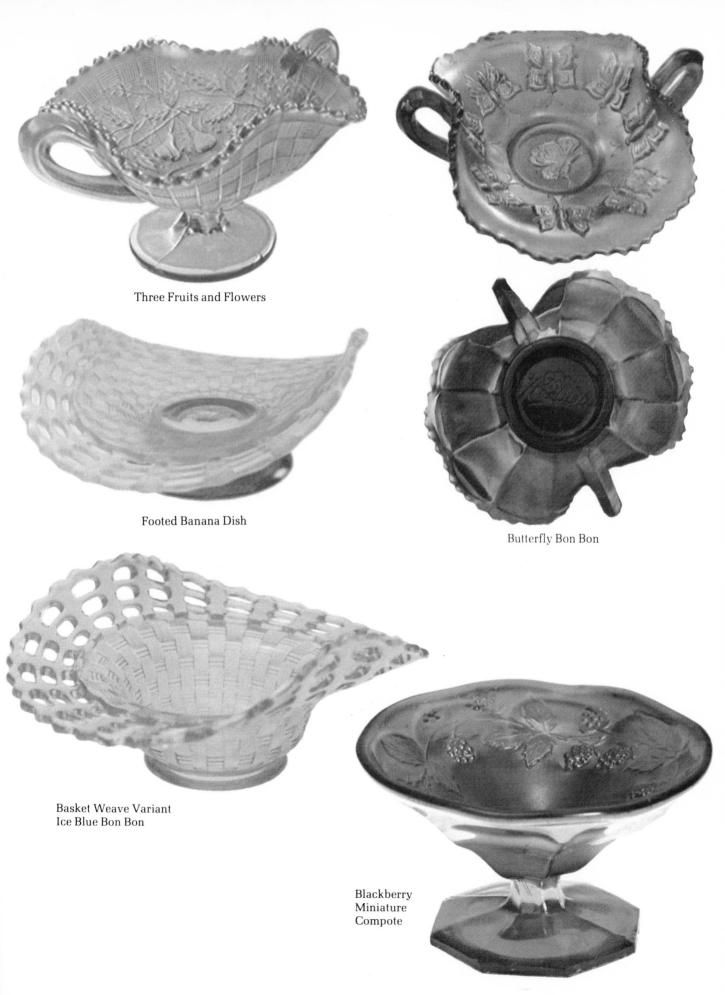

Three Fruits and Flowers

Footed Banana Dish

Butterfly Bon Bon

Basket Weave Variant
Ice Blue Bon Bon

Blackberry
Miniature
Compote

ROSE WREATH FOOTED BON BON

It is surprising how any of these footed candy dishes survived. Perhaps grandmother put these in the china cabinet from where they were brought out on special occasions. This one was made by Fenton.

FINE CUT AND ROSES BON BON

This was a rose bowl before the worker flared out the top. It has the interior pattern, Northwood's Fancy. The interior pattern is usually found inside the ice blue rose bowls, and sometimes the white ones but rarely in the purple. Most of these have the (N) in the bottom.

PUZZLE FOOTED BON BON

Another candy dish, this one we believe to be by Northwood though not marked. This one in amethyst. It could be mistaken for red. Here again we don't have the cherry red but a slightly over-balanced amethyst. The outside of this is the Floral and Wheat pattern.

Rose Wreath
Footed
Bon Bon

Fine Cut and Roses Bon Bon

The Puzzle
Footed
Bon Bon

RASPBERRY SAUCE BOAT

This has been referred to many times as a creamer, but never having seen a sugar to match, we believe it was a loner. Northwood was known for novelties. This is a typical basket weave around the bottom. It has the (N) in the bottom.

PANEL AND THUMBPRINT

These small compotes are usually referred to as jelly compotes. However, in the old trade catalogs we find most of them listed as footed mint dishes. What you wish to call them does not matter. If you like them, collect them. This has no marks but we think it is Northwood.

FOOTED SHELL MINT DISH

These are more of a novelty than anything else, especially the smaller one. They have a flat ground spot on the bottom, sometimes polished, but I can assure you this is not a pontil mark. These were pressed, and the legs or feet were so short that they had to grind off the bottom so the pieces would sit somewhere near level. However, they are very attractive and a little difficult to find.

Raspberry
Sauce Boat

Panel and
Thumb Print

Footed Shell
Mint Dish

CURVED STAR FLOWER HOLDER

Quite often you see these in china decorated with flowers and other designs, occasionally in clear crystal glass. We have seen only a couple of these in Carnival. They were both in marigold, though I am sure there were more colors. I doubt if they were made in any great quantity. There are no marks and we don't know the maker.

FLOWER FROG

This is much larger than the little fellow you find so often. This one is 1⅝ inches high and 4¼ inches wide. It has one one-inch hole in the center and eight half-inch holes surrounding the center hole. These could be used in any bowl large enough to hold them. Now they are sometimes used as paper weights.

VINTAGE EPERGNE

Not as large by any means as the Wide Panel shown in Book 1. This one is only 4¾ inches tall and 6 inches across. It is still very attractive and highly collectible. It may be found in marigold and blue. It was made by Fenton.

Curved Star
Flower Holder

The Flower
Frog

Vintage
Epergne

127

THE CORN BOTTLE

This bottle delights the eye of the bottle collector for many reasons. It looks like a small ear of corn and is exceptionally well done, usually having excellent color and iridescence. It is only 5" high and may be found in white and smoke, as well as green, marigold and purple.

COLONIAL PATTERN CHILD'S CANDLE-HOLDER

Children's pieces are always in demand. Perhaps too many of the pieces did not survive and the records are so sketchy of the companies that made children's pieces that a guess at the manufacturer would be pure conjecture. Anyway, we think this is quite nice. It measures 4½" high and 4½" across. Since it is the only one that I have seen, it is hard to say if it might be found in other colors.

GOLDEN WEDDING SALESMAN'S SAMPLE BOTTLE

We have heard all sorts of conflicting reports about small Carnival Glass bottles containing alcohol that we didn't believe. But we think this one did, though not too many of the little bottles survived the years. It is 3¾" high — probably held about 2 oz.

PERFUME BOTTLE

At first glance this little perfume bottle is similar to many others until you notice the stopper with the applicator with its small green leaves and the flower with the lavender petals. That makes it a little bit different — more like you would expect for milady. This was a commercial product — could have been made by any company. Cambridge Glass Company made many bottles for DeVilbis.

SODA GOLD CUSPIDOR

Not quite as dainty as the Ladies' Swirl Hobnail Cuspidor. These are always collectible in brass or china, so it is no wonder they are prized even more highly in Carnival Glass. This is 7 inches across and 4 inches high. These are usually found in marigold, but occasionally you may find one in green. They were made by Imperial.

ILLINOIS DAISY TOBACCO JAR

Covered jars have always been collectors' favorites. This one has been called a tobacco jar, which was its probable use. It doesn't have the fingers we find inside the cover of the Grape and Cable tobacco jar. We wouldn't venture a guess as to the manufacturer.

The Corn Bottle

Colonial Pattern
Childs Candleholder

Golden Wedding
Salesman's Sample
Bottle

Perfume Bottle

Spider Web and Soda
Gold Cuspidor

Illinois Daisy
Tobacco Jar

CANADA DRY BOTTLE

These are found quite frequently, probably not too often with the original label still intact, "Sparkling Orangeade with Natural Fruit Pulp." The top label reads, "Turn upside down before opening. Contains orange juice, aroma of the peel, a dash of lemon juice, pure cane sugar and carbonated water." It is believed these were made in 1923 by Northwood to commemorate some special event for the Canada Dry people.

BOSTON WINE BOTTLE

Due to the increased interest and activity in bottle collecting, we decided to include a few in this book. This one came from the New England Wine Company, Inc., of Boston, Mass. The cap is missing as usual. However, if you like bottles you will probably enjoy this one. They can still be found, and usually the price is not too high. It is marked on the bottom, "New England Wine Co., Boston, Mass."

THE JACKMAN WHISKEY BOTTLE

This one apparently wasn't as popular as the Golden Wedding bottle. We find dozens of the former to one of these. This little fellow usually demands more money although the color and iridescence are about the same. Of course these are all in the late category, after prohibition was repealed.

THE GOLDEN WEDDING WHISKEY BOTTLE

These are fairly common yet collectible. This one is somewhat different because of the cap. The cap is large enough to measure a shot or an ounce of liquid. I don't think that would add much if any to its value, but it is something we don't see every day.

Canada Dry
Bottle

Boston Wine
Bottle

The Jackman
Whiskey Bottle

The
Golden Wedding
Whiskey Bottle

THE BARBER'S BOTTLE

We kind of like this bottle, although the marigold only comes down about half way. The Little Mellon Rib pattern may add to its attractiveness. This has good iridescence all over. It was probably made by the Cambridge Glass Company. One of the former employees told me they made some bottles and candy containers in iridescent glass for commercial use.

PERFUME BOTTLE WITH APPLICATOR

Devilbis had atomizers by the hundreds, but this is different. It has a long stopper with a little knob on the end, just right for putting a drop of perfume behind milady's ear. There are no marks, again a commercial item, probably by Cambridge.

PROUD PUSS DECANTER

This was a useful as well as a decorative piece, for it had its own shot glass on top. Children would see the resemblance to Dr. Seusse's cat in the hat character. It is in good heavy glass with good iridescence. Too bad we don't know who the maker was. Our gratitude to the Ripley's.

FRUIT JAR

It is no surprise to find this Ball Mason canning jar. The surprise is why we don't find more of them. In all my travels I have only seen a couple. Just what is the object of their iridescence is anybody's guess — perhaps to preserve the food better, would be mine.

HORN-OF-PLENTY BOTTLE

It seems that everybody had a turn at the whiskey bottles in Carnival Glass. Lord Calvert was no different. This one came out about 1933 soon after the repeal of Prohibition. It is a commercial item, so any glass company could have made it.

The Barber's
Bottle

Perfume Bottle
With Applicator

Proud Puss
Decanter

Fruit Jar

Horn-of-Plenty Bottle

CONCAVE DIAMOND PICKLE CASTOR

Everything indicates this to be a rare one. Though I am sure I will hear of more of these as soon as this book is circulated, so far we have seen only two besides the one shown. We find the pattern a little more often in water sets or lemonade sets, most always in ice blue. Usually the top or cover of the pitcher is missing. We don't know about the castor sets, but the lemonade sets were given away for X number of punches on the Jewel Tea cards, so this may also have been a commercial item.

WIDE PANEL EPERGNE

This lovely piece was originally called a combination fruit and flower holder, as the original catalog listing shows.

But times have changed. Neither fruit nor flower would enhance the beauty of this creation.

There were no manufacturer's identifying marks. The wide panel was often used by Northwood, Fenton and Imperial and less often by Westmorland.

As one might guess, the four-lily epergne is more difficult to find than a single-lily but either is worth the search.

The original listing
as reproduced from the
Baltimore Bargain Book, 1912.

**"IRIDESCENT" COMBINATION
FRUIT AND FLOWER HOLDER,**

Used as Table
Centerpiece.

Magnificently decorative. The exclusive principles of the expensive imported ware maintained throughout—they differ only in price.

1C2116 — 11 in. fluted bowl shape fruit receptacle base, 4 removable lily design bouquet holders, emerald green glass cleverly enriched with rainbow hued iridescent tones. 1 in case, 30 lbs.

Each, **$1.35**

Concave Diamond Pickle Castor

Wide Panel Epergne

SMOOTH PANEL DECANTER

Likely this was intended for whiskey or brandy, however we have never seen any glasses we could associate with this decanter. It is 12" high and 4" wide, and has no marks to identify the maker.

WHISKEY BOTTLE

Carnival Glass bottles are not easy to come by. especially in dark. This one is a dark amber and iridescence is very good. On the side of the bottle is the following: "25 3/5 ounces," and on the bottom there is what appears to be the letter W in a triangle.

MELON RIB CORDIAL SET

This little set probably had 6 of the glasses though we only show 4. The decanter is 10¼" high to the top of the stopper and 3¼" wide. The glasses are 3½" high and close to 1½" wide at the top. They tell me these were made about the mid-Twenties. Maker is unknown.

Smooth Panel Decanter

Whiskey Bottle

Melon Rib Cordial Set

MAPLE LEAF HANDLED BASKET

This is a very unusual basket, rather flat, yet very attractive. It has the beaded heart pattern on the exterior, which leads us to believe it was made by Northwood. It is about 8″ across and the handle is about 6″ high — and it may have come in other colors. Our thanks to Jack Burk of Pipestone, Minn.

CURVED STAR CHALICE

This piece is unique in many ways. The pattern is well adapted to this shape. It looks as though it might be a vase or even a celery, but they tell me it is a chalice, and it does resemble some I have seen in church. This is 6½″ high and 5″ across. Shown here in marigold, it may also be found in blue. These are not too plentiful. Maker is unknown.

COLONIAL CANDLESTICKS

This is one of the things we can collect and use even today. This particular set is not too expensive and yet very attractive. Most all the glass companies made this Colonial and Wide Panel, so it is anybody's guess who made these.

CURVED STAR CANDLESTICK

A very unusual candleholder or candlestick, whichever you prefer to call it. It is a very deep marigold color with excellent iridescence. 11″ high, it measures 5″ wide at the bottom.

SAINT CANDLESTICK

You see these occasionally in clear glass but I believe they are rare in Carnival Glass. You who have seen them in clear, will notice right away that someone has cut off the part the candle sat in. A guess at the manufacturer would be pure conjecture. Thanks to the Ripley's.

Maple Leaf Basket

Curved Star Chalice

Colonial Candlesticks

Curved Star Candlestick

Saint Candlestick

FINE RIB FIVE LILY EPERGNE

This epergne is far different than the Wide Panel epergne. This one was just for flowers only while the Wide Panel was a combination fruit and flower holder. Northwood made a Fine Rib lily and some of the Rib shades for lighting fixtures, but who may have made the final assembly is anybody's guess. There were numerous jobbers who purchased glass parts from one company and metal parts from another and marketed them under their own name, just the same as they did with the lamps, in many cases.

THE INVERTED FEATHER CRACKER JAR

Although Grape and Cable is more avidly sought for a cracker jar, this pattern is still a highly collectible item and a good conversation piece.

It is found mostly in green, which hints of Fenton or Millersburg.

THE JARDINIERE

There is deep and compelling mystery about this item. It probably was purely for decoration since its size (6″) and shape wouldn't hold very much, perhaps pencils. I lean toward Fenton as the maker of the few pieces.

Fine Rib 5 Lilly Epergne

Inverted Feather Cracker Jar

The Jardiniere

CHILD'S HICKMAN CASTOR SET

This should delight the hearts of the miniature collectors'! We think this little cruet, salt dip and shaker are just great. Not like some of the others, this one has good color and good iridescence. Our many thanks to Marilyn Gaida of Victoria, Texas.

PENNY MATCH HOLDER

This holder is rather hard to come by. It was made so that a penny box of matches would slip over the top part and leave the box open enough to remove a match. These are found mostly in dark. My guess is that they would be extremely rare in marigold. Maker unknown. Again thanks to the Ripley's.

SODA GOLD URN

This urn was no doubt a commercial item and supposedly contained orange juice. Possibly not suited for a container it was soon abandoned, which could be a good explanation of why there are so few around. However, be it fact or fiction, it is something different and quite nice for a collection of rare and unusual pieces.

SCROLL PIN TRAY

We don't know if there were other pieces with this, but the collector of miniatures and other small pieces will surely find a spot for one of these. It is 1" high × 6" long and 2½" wide.

SWEETHEART COOKIE JAR

Covered dishes and especially jars are desirable in most any glass, but more so in Carnival and in the larger sizes. This is one of the nicest ones I have seen. This jar is about 9" tall and about 6" at the widest point. Occasionally you see one of these in clear glass which leads me to think there are more to be found in more colors. There are no marks to identify the maker.

BUD VASE WHIMSEY

The collector who likes the different and unusual things would surely enjoy this little bud vase. Just what the glass worker had in mind when he shaped this Whimsey, I really don't know — whatever it was I love it. This is cobalt blue and has fine iridescence. It is 5½" high at the tallest point and 5½" at the widest.

Hickman Castor Set

Penny Match Holder

Soda Gold Urn

Scroll Pin Tray

Sweetheart Cookie Jar

Bud Vase Whimsey

CARNIVAL BELL

I'm quite sure this bell was made to commemorate some event at Graceville, Minnesota. These souvenir pieces were often given at such occasions. There is no way as to even guess who the manufacturer may have been.

COLONIAL TOOTHPICK HOLDER

This 2-handled toothpick item is different than the Wide or Flute Toothpick Holder. This piece measures 2¼″ high and is 3¾″ across the extreme edges of the handles. The color is good and the iridescence very good for this type. It was made by Imperial and marked with the old Iron Cross.

VIOLET BASKET

We have seen many of these little hat-shaped dishes, but we never made the connection until we found this one in the metal holder. Then it dawned on us why they had the little indentations on the side — for the handle! We think most were made by Northwood, though none we have ever seen were marked, however, the band near the top is very much the same as some of the Stork and Rushes.

TWO HANDLED SALT DIP

Here is another cutie, though it has no pattern. Maybe the shape of it makes it so attractive. When we look back and think of the tons of glass that were broken in the old cast iron sinks, it seems a miracle that a small delicate piece such as this could survive.

WIDE PANEL FOOTED SALT DIP

We have seen several different pieces that people refer to as master salt dips. Often we disagree, but this one we feel sure was used for that purpose. The wide panel would tell you right away it is Northwood, but this one does have the (N) in the center. It probably came in all colors.

FLOWER POT

Flower pots were usually made of clay or pottery, but apparently they made some out of Carnival Glass also. I have seen one more besides this one, and I am sure there are others. This leads me to believe that Carnival was the most versatile of all types of glass. This piece is 5 inches high and 4¾ inches wide and has a half-inch hole in the bottom.

BANDED DIAMOND AND FAN TOOTHPICK

Here's another pattern that goes way back to when the sizes were more generous. The piece is about 3¼″ high by 2¼″ wide. Probably made by Westmoreland. Thank you Rosalie White.

Carnival Bell

Colonial Toothpick Holder

Violet Basket

Two Handled Salt Dip

Wide Panel Footed Salt Dip

Flower Pot

Banded Diamond and Fan Toothpick

GRAPE AND CABLE COVERED DISHES

Covered dishes, especially if the covers are intact, set a collector's heart to throbbing. If these don't, I give up!

First there are the tobacco jars, one in marigold, one in purple. These may also be found in other colors, but not quite so readily. There are three fingers in the lid to hold a sponge.

The large covered compote — 9″ tall and 6½″ across — is usually found in amethyst and is very rare in marigold, as shown here. It would be a wonderful find in ice-blue or ice-green, however I still feel they were probably made in all the colors.

The cookie jar, easily identified because it has the handles, is almost common in marigold and amethyst. It is shown here in aqua-opalescent which is quite rare. Though I have seen it in ice-blue and in white, this is the first and only aqua-opalescent. I am sure there are more in this color.

The sweet-meat compote is easy to identify because it is much smaller and has the cathedral top. This one is usually found in amethyst and an occasional cobalt blue, sometimes even in green. Right now the marigold is the expensive one. They probably came in white, though none have shown up yet. Several have been seen in clear, but are not iridized. Are they out there some-where?

Almost all of these have the famous N in the bottom, and sometimes even on the underside of the cover. Our thanks to the Moores and the Williams for the loan of these pieces.

Grape and Cable Tobacco Jars

Grape and Cable Large Covered Compote

Grape and Cable Cookie Jar

Grape and Cable Sweetmeat Compote

MILLERSBURG BUTTERMILK GOBLET

This is a little larger than most of the goblets but in those days they were a little more generous. Remember the Grape and Cable shot glasses one and one-half times the size of the standard shot glass of today. The Iris pattern on the inside very much resembles the Heavy Iris. These may be found in green and also in amethyst.

SAILBOAT WINE GLASS

Perhaps this was just an occasional wine glass. I don't recall seeing a decanter that would match it. Nevertheless it is quite nice and a collector's favorite. This was made by Fenton. The cobalt blue is the most sought after. There also is a goblet in this pattern.

IMPERIAL GRAPE CUP AND SAUCER

Cups and saucers are uncommon, even in late Carnival. This is *early* Carnival Glass and is extremely rare.

The *old* Imperial Grape still is high on collectors' lists. It led in popularity at the time it was made, also.

The saucer is an exclusive Carnival pattern.

THE IMPERIAL GRAPE GOBLET

The authentic old goblets have been reproduced but never equaled.

They have the pattern on the inside AND outside, the color is more delicately shaded and the many-rayed star on the foot is distinctive.

This is a collector's find.

Millersburg Buttermilk Goblet

Sailboat Wine Glass

Imperial Grape Cup and Saucer

Imperial Grape Goblet

DRESSER BOTTLES

Not on every shopping trip do you find Carnival Glass bottles. Less often you find a matched pair. These have gold trim. The lettering on one reads "Hand Lotion" and on the other "Astringent". I believe the latter was used for closing the pores of the skin and removing excess oils. The bottles are 2½ inches square and 4½ inches high. The stoppers are solid. They are a good rich marigold. The gold trim and the lettering show wear, but the iridescence is still very good, which indicates the iridescence will take more wear and abuse than the gold or painted enamels. Again this is a commercial item with not much chance of tracing the manufacturer.

INSULATOR

Many people collect insulators, so maybe some of you will enjoy seeing this one. It has a skirt-like flare, for what reason I am not sure. It was made at Corning and is numbered. Why it is not like the rest is anybody's guess.

TRACERY DOT PERFUME ATOMIZER

The interesting thing about this bottle is that it probably cost more than the perfume that came in it. These dots were cut after the iridescence was applied to the bottle. Also the lines were cut afterwards. There are no marks or clue to the maker, which is often the case with commercial pieces.

WESTERN HAT (L.B.J.)

I haven't the slightest idea who named this the L.B.J. Hat. However, it is worthy of a famous name. We don't have the complete history of this, but we have been told it was made to compliment western cattlemen or cowboys. This is a much earlier piece than a lot of people think. It was probably intended for an ash tray but used primarily as decorative.

Dresser Bottles

ASTRINGENT

HAND LOTION

Insulator

Tracery Dot
Perfume Atomizer

CORNING PYREX TM.REG...

The Western Hat (L.B.J.)

GRAPE AND CABLE CANDLE LAMPS

Candle lamps are in short supply, and one look would be sufficient to see why. The shade holder fits over the candle, so all that holds it is the small amount of candle that fits down in the candlestick. It is possible to find bases, but the fragile character of the glass shades made survival through 50 or more years of handling and storage something miraculous. These were made by Northwood and the candlesticks most always have the N mark, but the shades are never marked. Green is the most common color, purple and marigold are more scarce.

ZIPPER-LOOP LAMPS

Oil lamps have been collectable for some time now and these are no exception. Shown here in three different sizes, with the large sewing lamp being easiest to acquire, the middle sized lamp not really that easy to come by, and the little fellow, the hand lamp, seems to be in very limited supply. These were made by the Imperial Glass Company, and they did reissue some of the larger ones for a short while, but apparently gave it up. The reissues were marked the the I.G. — a superimposed "I" running through a capital "G". These were made mostly in marigold, with an occasional one in smoke color.

CANDLE SHADE HOLDERS.

AO1704—Fit any candle shade, length 4½ in., extends to 7 inches, spring clamp; 1 doz. in box....doz., **35c**

AO1705—Height 4¼ inches, nickel finish, weighted holder, fits over candle and adjusts itself as candle burns; 1 doz. in box, doz., **65c**

CRYSTAL GLASS CANDLESTICKS.

Shade holder listing from catalog of the Baltimore Bargain House, April, 1912

Grape and Cable Candle Lamps

Zipper-Loop Lamps

RIB AND SWIRL LAMP SHADE

This is a typical 10″ shade. The color is just a trifle darker than the ice-blue. Fenton made a light blue very similar to this. The iridescence is very good on this piece, however, this shade did not come on this lamp. There were a pair of these shades and one got broken. I am sure they were on a double Student Lamp.

THE MILLERSBURG LAMP

The Millersburg lamp (opposite) is a typical Carnival lamp with one exception. On the underside of the base is impressed medallions of three ladies. These are reported to be the wives of three major stockholders of the Millersburg Glass Company. The lamp was found in the Amish district near the factory. The owners thought it also had been made in marigold and red.

The pattern is known as Wild Rose and Honeycomb, also as Blossom and Band.

Rib and Swirl Lamp Shade

Millersburg Lamp

THE HAMMERED BELL CHANDELIER

Rare, indeed, is the word for a chandelier of this type — the hammered bell chandelier.

I have often wondered why one never appeared with the original clapper. The few encountered had no clapper or had a bead attached with a wire. One or two had a prism, but none appeared to be original equipment.

The Ripleys of Indianapolis found this one in a small antique shop. Luckily, the owners were not aware of the value of the hammered bell shades or they would have dismantled the chandelier and sold each bell separately. We might never have known its intended use.

Quite frankly, I don't know who the manufacturer was. Originally I guessed Fenton or Northwood until I talked to a man who cleaned molds for Fenton. He was certain that he never saw this particular pattern so, by elimination, it seems to be Northwood.

THE AUTUMN OAK CHANDELIER

Perhaps the artist who designed this pleasing pattern enjoyed the fall of the year. He endeavored to capture the golds, browns and reds of the season when acorns drop and the pumpkins ripen.

These shades, because of color and iridescence, strongly suggest Northwood origin.

Hammered
Bell
Chandelier

Autumn Oak
Chandelier

MOUNTAIN LAKE SCENE CHANDELIER

We thought this chandelier was very intriguing. It is difficult to be sure just what the artist had in mind with the limited space available, however, it is not difficult to tell that this was one of our great artists. The dome shade is a 10″ top fitter. There were four small matching shades, (not shown) The maker is unknown.

FLORAL AND SCROLL ETCHED LAMP SHADE

This is another type of the library table lamp. It was etched with acid, and then the iridescence was applied later. The inside of this shade is a shiny marigold that gives the appearance of late Carnival, but we don't think that is the case here. The former owner of this lamp tells us it was a wedding gift to the parents in 1912.

PORTABLE LAMP OR LIBRARY TABLE LAMP

We find this type of lamp advertised in the Rouss Catalog, March, 1914, as well as by Butler Bros. and Drummer. These were the early electric lamps, the first with cords and plugs. They could easily be moved from one table to another, wherever the electric outlet would be.

Almost every electric appliance or gadget is now portable, but I can assure you it was not always so. These were made with decorated shades, and what we call leaded shades, in great quantities, but we don't think a great many of them had Carnival shades such as the one we show you here. This is a typical marigold. The underside is a mite shiny but it does have good iridescence. The outside is a fine stippling, more like a sand finish. We find the same fine stippling on the Shell and Jewel Cream and Sugar set. Is it by Westmoreland? The marigold is almost the same color.

Mountain Lake Scene Chandelier

Floral and Scroll
Etched Lamp Shade

A Portable Lamp or
Library Table Lamp

SUNKEN HOLLYHOCK "GONE WITH THE WIND" LAMP

Reminiscent of the days of Rhett Butler and Scarlett O'Hara, this is one of the most valuable single pieces of Carnival Glass known.

Originally, it was purchased from a Pennsylvania farm couple for a few dollars and a large collection of Carnival was built around it.

Because of illness, the entire collection was sold and the lamp was transported to the west coast, then back. It survived an automobile mishap and finally was purchased for my collection at a newsworthy price, at that time far greater than had ever been paid for Carnival.

It is 25 inches tall. The ball shade is 10 inches in diameter. The pattern is known as Sunken Hollyhock which is understood to be exclusively a lamp pattern. It has been seen on red satin "Gone With the Wind" lamps.

REGAL IRIS, GONE-WITH-THE-WIND LAMP

This GWTW lamp is a collector's dream come true. It is one of the large lamps, with a 10″ ball shade and is about 25″ high. Exceptionally good color and iridescence. May be found in white and marigold, but rarely in red as shown here. From the collection of Mrs. Helen Greguire.

Sunken Hollyhock, Gone-With-the-Wind Lamp

Regal Iris, Gone-With-the-Wind Lamp

SHASTA DAISY

These Decorated Carnival Water Sets were shown in the old catalogues along with the other Carnival and were advertised as "Decorated Iridescent." This set we feel sure was made by Northwood, though the pitcher and the tumblers are not marked.

IRIS AND RIBBON DECORATED CARNIVAL

This is one of the more attractive of the decorated Carnival, which has gained in popularity over the past two years. There are no marks to identify the manufacturer of this lovely piece.

RIBBON AND DRAPE PITCHER

This lovely pitcher is very similar to the Iris and Ribbon, only this one has the drape pattern on the inside of the glass, much like the swirl-rib pattern water set. A guess at the manufacturer would be just that. Most of the glass companies decorated glass before Carnival came on the scene, so it is no wonder we find some of it now. There has been a great amount written about the other Carnival glass but, sadly, very little on the decorated Carnival glass.

FORGET-ME-NOT (VARIANT)

This is very similar to the Forget-Me-Not. Only the leaves and color are different. Copy or coincidence, the artist created a very pleasing effect. From the Greguire collection.

SECTION 6 — DECORATED CARNIVAL GLASS

Shasta Daisy Water Set

Iris and Ribbon

Ribbon and Drape

Forget-Me-Not (Variant)

FREESIA WATER SET

A very beautiful pitcher. Though the decorating doesn't measure up to some of the standards of the other Decorated Carnival Glass, it is still desirable and should not be passed up too lightly. At the present time we have no way of identifying the maker. From the Neroni collection.

CHERRIES AND BLOSSOMS WATER SET

Little has been written about this type of glass, and we haven't done nearly enough research, but we feel certain this set was made by Northwood because we saw one tumbler made with an N. However, there was only one tumbler in that set that was marked — and none of these are. Our thanks to Mr. and Mrs. Robert Neroni, of Rochester, N.Y.

MAGNOLIA AND DRAPE WATER SET

This is one of the nicest decorated water sets and is easy to identify. Most of the companies did some decorated art glass, but they did more of it before Carnival. It is very difficult to assign a piece to any particular company except for a few of the Northwood pieces which have the N mark on them. Regardless of who might have made it some of these pieces are nice and would enhance any collection.

MARY GREGORY WATER SET (COPY)

While we are showing Decorated Carnival (or Iridescent) Water Sets, we thought we would display this one because it is unique. It appears to be the same as the other Mary Gregory sets, with the exception of the iridescence. This does have a good iridescence. The pitcher is 8½″ high, 3¼″ across the top, and 5″ wide at the bottom. The glasses or tumblers are 5″ high and 2¼″ wide.

Freesia Water Set

Cherries and Blossoms Water Set

Magnolia and Drape Water Set

Mary Gregory Water Set

MARY GREGORY TYPE DRESSER BOTTLES

These dresser bottles were sometimes referred to as Barber bottles, but we don't agree. We think they were more apt to be found on a lady's dresser. We were told that one bottle contained cologne and the other astringent, but to date cannot authenticate this. Note that this has a different decoration than the Mary Gregory Water Set shown elsewhere in the book. No doubt a different manufacturer. Our thanks to Rosalie White, Springfield, Mo.

PANELED ASTOR CRUET, DECORATED

This is something very different in cruets. There may or may not have been more pieces with this item. It is 5″ in height and 3¼″ wide. Marked with an H, and an A in the bottom of the H, — I assume Hazel Atlas Glass Company.

DECORATED ALENCON LACE TOOTHPICK

One of the finer pieces in Decorated Carnival Glass. And one of the more generous sizes (3″ high by 2″ wide). Our thanks to Mrs. Rosalie White for lending us this lovely piece.

Mary Gregory Type Dresser Bottles

Paneled Astor Cruet

Alencon Lace Toothpick

HOB-STAR AND FEATHER GIANT ROSE BOWL

Everybody loves rose bowls, so I am quite sure you will enjoy this one, which can easily be classed as a giant rose bowl. It is about the same size as the Venetian giant rose bowl which is 9¼″ high and 5½″ wide and it weighs 5 pounds. This is a deep amethyst and the iridescence is fantastic. It seems a pity that the Millersburg Glass Company had to go out of business, when they could make such beautiful glass.

VENETIAN GIANT ROSE BOWL

This is another piece you would know at a glance was Millersburg. It is a typical Millersburg green and has fine iridescence. We have seen this one in marigold and it was just as lovely. We dug up pieces of it at the old Millersburg plant — even some pieces in clear glass, but at the time we had not yet encountered the giant rose bowl and were somewhat confused as to what it could be. Needless to say, we were delighted to find the giant rosebowl, because that solved our mystery. Both of these pieces are now in the collection of Don and Connie Moore and our thanks again to them for the privilege of their use in this book.

WIDE PANEL GIANT ROSE BOWL

The giant rose bowls were at one time popular. In early Victorian photos, the giant rose bowl can sometimes be seen on the bottom post of the stairway. By the time Carnival came on the scene, they had lost a lot of their favor. We don't believe there were too many of them made, and today they are a find. We suspect this was made by Northwood.

STAG AND HOLLY GIANT ROSE BOWL

Like the Horse Medallion, this Stag and Holly pattern is on the inside of the bowl. It is also made by Fenton, who made most of our animal pieces. These are rather scarce, especially in green or blue. They possibly came in white and amethyst, but more often in marigold.

Section 7 — Rose Bowls, Mugs and Baskets

Hob-Star and Feather Giant Rose Bowl

Venetian Giant Rose Bowl

Wide Panel Giant Rose Bowl

Stag and Holly Giant Rose Bowl

LEAF AND BEADS, BEADED CABLE, DRAPERY

These are all Northwood and may be found in the usual colors plus the aqua-opalescent shown here. Perhaps the reason this color is so difficult to find is that just before Carnival glass came on the scene there had been a big run of opalescent glass. Housewives were tired of opalescent glass and wanted something different, so they apparently didn't buy much aqua-opalescent Carnival glass. Not much of it was made, therefore today you have to pay dearly to get a piece of aqua-opalescent.

SWIRL HOBNAIL, HONEYCOMB, HOBNAIL

These are all Millersburg pieces. The Swirl Hobnail was probably made from the same mould that was used for the cuspidor, or vice-versa. Anyway, it is an attractive rose bowl and highly collectable. It may be found in amethyst or green as well as the marigold shown here.

The Honeycomb in peach opalescent may have only come in the one color, though other colors are possible. It is said that these were made for one of the principal stockholders in the Millersburg Company to pack honey in, as he was a beekeeper. Whether this is fact or fiction I can neither confirm or deny, but whatever the intended use, it is now highly collectable.

The Hobnail is like the Swirl Hobnail only it doesn't have the swirl, and may be found in the same colors. The choice is strictly a matter decided by the collector.

FENTON'S LITTLE FLOWERS

As the flowers are smaller than you see on large bowls and plates, you might mistake this pattern for the Orange Tree, but a close look will tell you it is the Little Flowers pattern. It came in most of the usual colors — more often in marigold and blue, but it also may be found in green and, on rare occasions, in white.

HORSE MEDALLION

Very unique, we think, and this pattern was no doubt inspired by the famous painting by John F. Herring, a British artist, entitled "Pharoah's Horses". This is another of Fenton's animal patterns and is usually found in marigold and blue, though other colors are possible.

GRAPE DELIGHT

This is the only rosebowl we have run across with six feet in the Carnival glass field. It is shown here in amethyst, but comes in blue, white and marigold. There are no marks to identify the manufacturer.

Leaf and Beads

Beaded Cable

Drapery

Swirl Hobnail

Honeycomb

Hobnail

Fenton's Little Flowers

Horse Medallion

Grape Delight

FISHERMAN'S MUG

The Fisherman's mug at one time contained peanut butter, and sometimes they were used as a souvenir piece also. We had one that had compliments of a grocery in Harrisburg, Pennsylvania inscribed on the back side. The dark one, when held to the sun or a strong light, looks red. But like some of the other pieces, marigold is the favorite, because there are not many of them, so the scarcity of them drives the price up. Although there are no markings, we strongly suspect these were made by Fenton.

BEADED SHELL MUG

Despite the fact that there is no N on either of these mugs, it is Northwood's, and like the Fisherman's mug, the marigold is the hard one to find, so that seems to govern the price.

SINGING BIRD MUG

The Singing Bird mugs almost always have the famous N in the bottom and are most often found in marigold and amethyst, but also in blue and in green, which is considered rare. The ice-blue and the aqua-opalescent are even more rare. Northwood made the lion's share of those colors and I am surprised that more have not been found. Regardless of color, one of these is a must for the mug collector.

ORANGE TREE MUG

The Orange Tree mugs were made by Fenton and apparently came in all the colors they normally made. These are most often found in marigold and blue, but sometimes in amethyst and green, and if you are lucky, you might find one in white or even red. This came in two different sizes, the regular drinking mug and the larger shaving mug. (Note the difference in size.) The shaving mug probably was not made in the same quantities as the drinking mug. I have seen only a couple, and they were blue, though they may have come in other colors.

LITTLE BO-PEEP MUG

The Little Bo-Peep mug shown here is believed to be one of Northwood's experimental pieces, made before he mastered the art of iridizing. The color is bad and the iridescence has a lot to be desired. We have a Grape and Cable powder jar made the same way — it has the N in the bottom. This mug is more often found in marigold and most of them have poor iridescence and the color was also poor. Only a few have had good color and iridescence. These are really scarce — you don't find one on every shopping trip.

BANDED GRAPE MUG

The Banded Grape is not too common. It may have come in different colors. Usually when you do see one it is marigold. There are no marks or any clue as to the maker.

STORK AND RUSHES

The Stork and Rushes is Northwood, marked or unmarked. Usually it came in marigold, but may also be found in blue — perhaps in amethyst and green.

HERON MUG

The Heron mug is something else! This one is definitely rare in any color, though I believe you will see more in blue than in amethyst or green — occasionally in marigold — but not many in any color.

Fisherman's Mugs

Beaded Shell Mugs

Singing Bird Mugs

Orange Tree Mugs

Little Bo-Peep Mug

Banded Grape Mug and Stork and Rushes Mug

Heron Mug

BUTTERFLY AND BERRY HAT-PIN HOLDER

"Milady" would have little use for these today other than as decorations, but not when these were made. She must have felt a lot of pride when she got one of these to sit on her dresser to hold those nice hat pins. We don't think there were any other pieces that went with these. We think there was just the one piece, and for the one purpose. These were made by the Fenton Art Glass Co.

LOVING CUPS

We thought that as we were showing small vases, we would feature the loving cup also. However, these loving cups have only two handles — not like the earlier loving cups (not Carnival) which had three handles. We think these are quite nice and are highly desirable in any collection. Shown here in blue, white, green and marigold, they may also be found in purple. The Orange Tree pattern would tell us that this is a Fenton product.

MARY ANN VASES

Like the Orange Tree Loving Cups, these are small vases. Sizes vary, though most of them are just over six inches high, while the loving cups are usually just under six inches. Marigold must have been the accepted color for these, though occasionally you will find one in amethyst, but not many, and we do have one in opalescent glass, not iridized. We did see one, and only one, of these in marigold with three handles. Unfortunately, we don't have it to show, but it did have good color and iridescence.

CORN VASE

Vases were made by the barrel in many sizes and colors, but few surpassed the Corn vase shown here. These are Northwood and as you might suspect, they are not all marked with the N. The Corn vase again reverses the usual pattern of collecting. In most cases, the pastels are favored over the dark and marigold, but not so in this instance. The marigold is probably tops, with the dark green and the amethyst following closely, then the pastels. There seem to be quite a few of these around, and they are highly desirable. If one is offered for sale, it is quickly picked up by a collector.

TRACERY BON-BON

This Tracery pattern is rather busy yet very attractive and not often found for sale. This is rather large for a bon-bon. It measures 6½" square and almost 5" high. Perhaps the Cosmos adds to its beauty. This was made by Millersburg and shown here in a typical Millersburg green, but it may also be found in marigold and amethyst in limited supply. It is in the Moore's collection.

DIAMOND POINT BASKET

These baskets were probably used more for nuts and candies than any other use and probably were more decorative than anything else. However, collectors have collected baskets a lot longer than I have been associated with glass, and this basket is definitely a dandy. The only thing, there are fewer of these to collect. Many people believe this was one of the last patterns produced at the Millersburg Glass Company before the plant closed down which would explain why there are not more of these available.

COSMOS AND CANE FOOTED ROSE BOWL

Not many rose bowls have a pedestal foot like this, though there are a few others, and like many more things, this was probably shaped from some other piece just to suit the glassmaker's taste. There are no marks to identify the maker, and too few to trace. Most people that have seen one of these think it was probably made by Cambridge Glass Company, which made so many containers. This cutie belongs to the Moore's.

Butterfly and Berry Hatpin Holders

Loving Cups

Mary Ann Vases

Corn Vases

Tracery Bon-Bon

Diamond Point Basket

**Cosmos and Cane
Footed Rose Bowl**

BUSHEL BASKET

LEFT

The Bushel Basket with the basketweave is Northwood's; most have the N in the bottom, and came in all colors. The white is usually shaped differently, with an eight-sided effect and flared a little more at the top. Particularly attractive is butterscotch color.

BIG BASKETWEAVE BUSHEL BASKET

RIGHT

The Big Basketweave Bushel Basket with two handles is more than likely Millersburg's, while the other Big Basketweave with the single handle is believed to be Fenton's. Either of these may be found in dark or marigold.

WAFFLE-BLOCK HI-HANDLED BASKET

LEFT

The Waffle-Block Hi-Handled basket may have come in all colors, but the marigold and clam-broth are more likely to be found.

DAISY HI-HANDLED BASKET

LEFT CENTER

The Daisy Hi-Handled basket is usually found in marigold. This one was Imperial's, and has been reissued, but the reissues should have an I.G. mark — the "I" running through the superimposed "G".

THE DIAMOND-HANDLED BASKET

RIGHT CENTER

The Diamond-Handled basket, or flat basket is rather unusual and was probably used as a mint dish. This basket was moulded like this. Many baskets had the handle applied, but this one was a one-piece mould. Having seen only this one, we don't know if there are other colors or how many were made.

THE CAROLINE BASKET

RIGHT

The Caroline, we think, was made from a bowl and the handle applied. Again, we have seen this only in the peach opalescent. There are no marks, though Northwood used the Caroline as a secondary pattern.

STORK AND RUSHES BASKET

LEFT

This was no doubt made from a tumbler. They flared out the top and applied the handle after it came from the mould. Some of the tumblers are marked on the bottom with an N, others are not. It is not known how many of these were made, but usually not many with this kind of piece, just a few for the glass worker and his friends and relatives. There is a good chance Mr. Northwood never saw these or else the glass worker might have looked for another place to work.

WIDE PANEL SALT-DIP BASKET

CENTER

This is probably a whimsey like the Stork and Rushes basket made at the Northwood plant, and probably was done while the boss wasn't looking. We find the N on most of the Wide Panel salt-dips, though not all of them, but we seldom find one that was made into a basket with a handle applied later. We think the glass worker strictly made these on his own and suspect very few were made.

THE BRITT, IOWA SOUVENIR BASKET

RIGHT

We think this basket was made from one of the round salt-dips and was made in a much larger quantity than the Wide Panel basket, however we are only guessing. So far, we have seen only one of the Britt, Iowa souvenir baskets, but we assume there were others made for different cities and towns, but are not in the hands of the collectors. Our thanks to Mrs. Britt for the loan of this piece.

Bushel Basket

Big Basket Weave Bushel Baskets

Diamond Handled and Caroline

Waffle-Block Hi-Handled and Daisy Hi-Handled

Stork and Rushes and Wide Panel Salt Dip Basket

Britt, Iowa Souvenir Basket

BIRD AND GRAPES WALL VASE

This is a good conversational piece. We all agree that they did hang on the wall, but the reason for them is not too clear. Some say flowers were placed in them, others say pencils, et cetera. Personally we think they were just decorative.

CAR VASE

They tell me this particular vase came out of a Packard Sedan. This should be more proof that at that time Carnival Glass was probably the leading art glass. They surely would have used what they thought was the most desirable for the fine automobiles of the day.

HAND VASE

The first time I encountered a vase of this sort was quite a few years ago; it was the same size but a different color — a pretty blue, however, it did not have the iridescence on it. This is one of the goodies of the old pressed glass, so you can imagine the thrill of finding one in Carnival! This vase is 5¼″ high and 2¾″ wide.

COMPOTE VASE

This is another piece more decorative than anything else. The coloring is good and the iridescence is fine. It is about 6 inches tall and flares out to about 4½ inches at the widest point at the top. This could have been a goblet. It has no pattern or mark, and there is no way of identifying it.

HERRING BONE AND IRIS VASE

These are thought to be Late Carnival, made in the late Twenties. Nevertheless the color and iridescence are good. The pattern is not quite as predominant as in some of the earlier pieces.

TORNADO VASES

Several vases sell for more money than this one, but few collectors ever part with it once they get one of these. This is a Northwood, sometimes marked. The marigold is the one most sought after in this particular item. It also comes in green and purple as shown here. May or may not be ribbed.

SECTION 8 — VASES AND OPEN COMPOTES

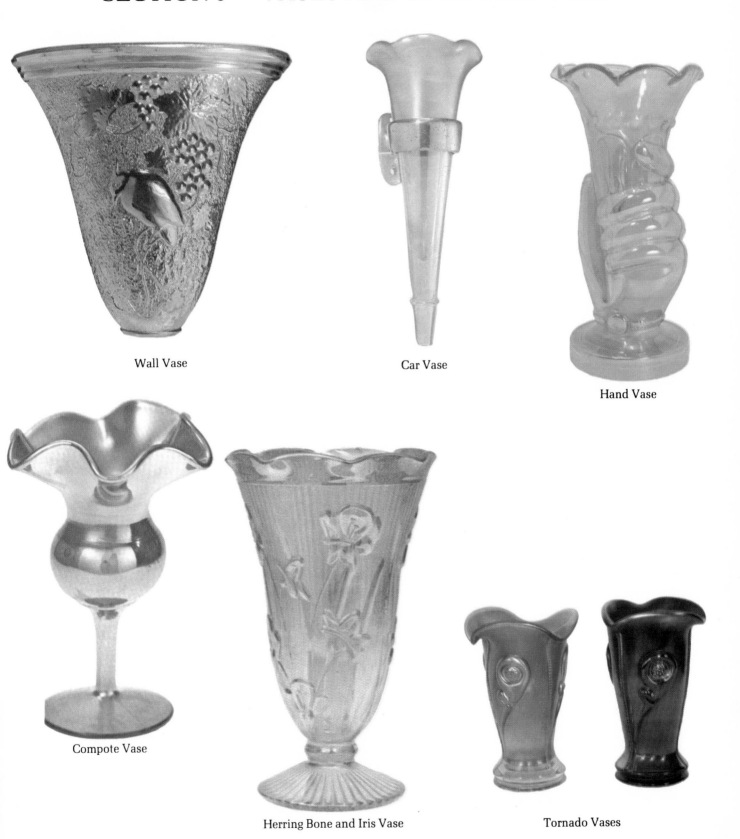

Wall Vase

Car Vase

Hand Vase

Compote Vase

Herring Bone and Iris Vase

Tornado Vases

LOGANBERRY VASE

Despite the fact that there have been some reissues of this particular piece, it is still one of the favorites of the collectors. Shown here in green, this is also attractive in other colors. This was made by the Imperial Glass Co.

POPPY VASE

Some people call this "The Poppy Show Vase." However, it is not the same pattern as the Poppy Show that is on the plates and bowls. This was also made by Imperial and there have been reissues, but the old ones are still a collector's favorite. The reissues would carry the IG mark.

RIB AND PANEL VASE, BLOWN

We usually try to avoid showing the same pattern more than once especially in the same book, but we are showing this only because they made a cuspidor out of the other one. Both of these pieces have the pontil mark on the bottom, so we feel sure they were blown. There are no identifying marks. From the Schleede's collection.

TREE TRUNK VASE

The size of this vase tells us it was a funeral vase — or at least it was intended to be. It is 12″ high and 9″ wide. However, it was never completed. If it had been slung out or stretched out it would have been about 20″ high, about the height of the other funeral vases. It does have the N. Our thanks to the Schleede's.

SUNFLOWER AND DIAMOND VASE

Here is one of the more desirable vases, and no doubt not too plentiful. It is thought to have been made by the Jenkins Glass Company, and I don't think they made nearly as much Carnival Glass as some of the other companies. From the Greguire collection.

MITERED OVALS VASE

This is one of the better vases made by the Imperial Glass Company. Though I haven't seen any reissues of this piece, the possibility still exists. However, if there were any, they would have the mark, which is the letter G with the superimposed I through the G. The vase is 10″ tall and 5½″ across. From the Greguire collection.

Loganberry Vase

Poppy Vase

Rib and Panel Vase

Tree Trunk Vase

Sunflower and Diamond Vase

Mitered Ovals Vase

COLONIAL VASE

This is a very simple pattern, but the shape makes it attractive. I don't think there is an abundance of these particular ones. I have seen them in green and marigold. Northwood made a pattern similar to this, but there is enough difference so that we think someone else made this one.

RIPPLE VASE

This vase comes in many different sizes and colors. Shown here is one of the larger ones measuring about 20 inches tall and roughly 7 inches across at the widest part. These larger ones were primarily used by funeral homes, and are often referred to as funeral vases. Of course they were not all used for that purpose. This is probably Imperial.

TALL HAT VASE

This piece will probably hold more interest for the collector that likes the pastels. This falls in the category of the Tall Hat and the Pastel Hat. These were believed given away by florists in an effort to increase their business during the heyday of Carnival Glass. As with many other commercial items, it would be next to impossible to identify the manufacturer.

INVERTED THUMBPRINT VASE

This large vase is very attractive perhaps mainly due to the shape. It is 8″ tall and 6½″ across the top. There are no marks to identify it. The Greguire collection.

JACK-IN-THE-PULPIT VASE

I think most of the major companies made some of these vases, but very seldom do you see one in peach opalescent. We thought this was very nice. So nearly all white with just a touch of the peach sets this apart from the rest. We think this is Imperial.

FORMAL VASE

A very attractive little vase with the thumbprints and the soda gold running the full length of the panels. We feel sure this is Imperial.

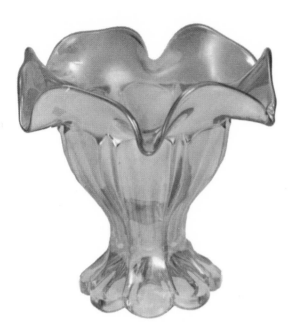

Colonial Vase

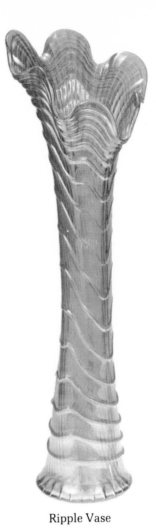

Ripple Vase

Tall Hat Vase

Inverted Thumbprint Vase

Jack in the Pulpit Vase

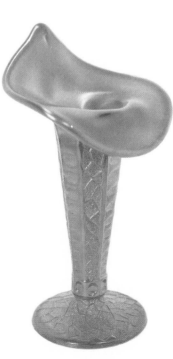

Formal Vase

GRAPE AND CABLE LARGE OPEN COMPOTE

This Grape and Cable compote is the most sought after of all the large open compotes, as they are usually hard to come by. I guess it came in most of the regular colors, though it is more often seen in green or amethyst than in marigold. There seems to be very few in white. Most collectors would be glad to settle for one in any color.

THE MIKADO LARGE OPEN COMPOTE

Large open compotes are rare and highly collectible.

Apparently, the manufacturers produced them in limited quantities because there is no reason for them not to survive as well as other pieces of this size.

Marigold is the most common color and the lowest price. I connect this to Fenton by the Cherry design.

PEACOCK AND URN LARGE OPEN COMPOTE

This large Open Compote has been attributed to Millersburg despite the fact there is beading on the Urn, which is not often found on the Millersburg Peacock & Urn, though some other Millersburg pieces do have the beading on the Urn. Shown here in amethyst, it also may be found in green as well as marigold, and again, the supply is very limited. From the Moore's collection.

THE INVERTED STRAWBERRY
Large Open Compote

There are jelly compotes, small compotes and medium compotes, but rarely does one find such a large one.

There is a "Near-Cut" inscription in the bottom of the bowl.

The wonderfully clear pattern was created by the Cambridge Glass Company and was widely used in the crystal and pressed glasses but there is no evidence of the company having made Carnival. The iridescence suggests Millersburg, but no records exist that credit it to that company.

Grape and Cable Large Open Compote

Mikado Large Open Compote

Peacock and Urn Compote

Large Inverted Strawberry
Open Compote and
Candlesticks

185

IMPERIAL'S WINDMILL AND FLOWERS TRAY

This brush and comb tray was another loner without any matching pieces to go with it. Imperial made several versions of the Windmill pattern for other pieces — bowls and plates, but few if any, carry this exact pattern. Shown here in purple, but may also be found in other colors.

THE SEAGULL

Here is something very unique in Carnival. The bird's head protrudes above the rim of the bowl. The lines in the glass give the effect of water which creates a very pleasing scene. It is a good quality glass and has good iridescence. I have seen it only in marigold.

IMPERIAL'S PANSY DRESSER TRAY

This tray was apparently just a large brush and comb tray without any matching dresser pieces to accompany it. Shown here in a true amber color, which was not used a lot in Carnival Glass. This may be found in green and marigold more readily than in amber or purple.

Imperial's Windmill and Flowers Tray

The Seagull

Imperial's Pansy Dresser Tray

VASES

WILD ROSE COMPOTE VASE

I know that most vases are considered to be of little value on the market, but the Wild Rose Compote is a masterpiece. Like the Farm Yard bowl, it was made after Northwood had absolutely mastered the art of applying iridescence and this example will rival Tiffany or Durand. It measures 8 inches across the top and is 5½ inches high. It is a deep purple, almost black, until held to the light. The iridescence is on the inside only.

ROCOCO

This Rococo design is too often overlooked, especially in marigold. The little fellow looks good any place. I would assign this to Imperial or Westmoreland. No matter which made it, the vase is worth seeking.

FAN VASE

The odd shape of The Fan Vase makes it attractive. It is believed that a worker at Millersburg made this as a personal experiment, something for his home or for a few friends. There is no evidence that it was marketed by the factory.

WISHBONE EPERGNE

The Wishbone Epergne is not quite as large as the Colonial Four Lily. It is a typical Northwood pattern although the (N) is missing. Note the basket weave on the exterior of the bowl. It is not easy to pass this one by. The marigold is very striking.

DAISY AND DRAPE

The Daisy and Drape is out of the ordinary. Like so many Northwood pieces, it may or may not be marked. It is equally attractive in all colors.

DIAMOND AND DAISY VASE

The Diamond and Daisy vase looks very much like some of the other vases from the outside, but the inside has a highly raised daisy on the bottom. If you find one of the short vases that was not slung-out, you will find the diamonds run horizontal instead of vertical. As the worker slung the vase he stretched out the diamonds to run up and down instead of around the vase. This is one of the things we learn as we study the art of making glass. Like many of the Northwood pieces, it may or may not be marked.

DAISY BLOCK ROWBOAT

Again we have a piece that was purely decorative. These are occasionally still found in the old pressed glass in both electric blue, and amber, but they are very hard to locate in Carnival Glass. I have seen one other in a good, rich marigold. Our thanks to Mr. and Mrs. Carl Schleede of Spencerport, N.Y. for this one.

PEACOCK-AT-THE-FOUNTAIN COMPOTE

You will find this pattern on punch bowls and berry sets, table sets, et cetera, but rarely find it in a compote — so we thought you would enjoy seeing it. It does have the N mark. From the Schleede's collection.

Rococo

Wild Rose Compote Vase

Fan

Wishbone

Daisy and Drape

Diamond and Daisy

Daisy Block Rowboat

Peacock at the Fountain

THE NAUTILUS

The Nautilus is a candy dish that was a passing fancy of Mr. Northwood and this, I believe, is the only piece in Carnival glass that carries this pattern. Many collectors will recognize it as the Argonaut Shell pattern, carried over from the opalescent and the custard glass days that preceded Carnival Glass. It is often found in amethyst, though occasionally found in peach-opalescent, but seems rather rare when found in another color. Some have been reported in green and in white, but the chances of finding one in those colors are most remote. These pieces are the only ones I have found that were signed in script "Northwood".

THE LITTLE BARREL

This is a very scarce item. I have heard all sorts of stories as to what this bottle contained.

Of the few I have encountered, all seem to have the stopper missing. Supposedly, the one shown here is an original stopper, it being a type used in that era. I am inclined to believe this. This bottle was purchased in a private home from a lady who originally received it as a Christmas gift. It contained perfume.

THE INSULATOR

The insulator is becoming quite a favorite and is often used as a paper weight. This one was made by the Corning Class Company, Corning, New York. The number is 63.

Iridescence was applied on these insulators supposedly to make them nonstatic. It apparently did not work because they soon resorted to other types.

Carnival insulators actually were used on power lines. The elements did not damage the iridescence. Evidently sun light does not fade or damage Carnival Glass.

THE PERFUME ATOMIZER

This little atomizer is very attractive even though there is no pattern. It seems quite remarkable that a small thing like this could survive and still be intact, including the rubber hose and the rubber ball. This piece is marked Devilbiss.

THE SEACOAST PIN TRAY

This little pin tray is a novelty, mainly because it is so attractive. It is quite different from other patterns. For one thing, the fish is much larger than the lighthouse. In the extreme left upper corner we can see a small sail boat and just to the right of the lighthouse we see the sun coming up which, all in all, creates a very pleasing effect.

It is seen in marigold, green and amethyst. The manufacturer is unknown.

THE SUNFLOWER PIN TRAY

This small pin tray measures almost 6″ the long way and not quite 4″ the short way, but what it lacks in size, it makes up other ways. When we see the Sunflower pattern in Carnival Glass we think of Northwood, but we can't authenticate it. Regardless of who made it, most anyone would be proud to have it in their collection in whatever color they found it.

THE WILDROSE SYRUP

My personal feeling is that this is an extremely rare piece of Carnival Glass. During the Carnival era syrups were a must. The trade catalogues listed them by the barrels in clear, crystal and cut but very few Carnival syrups were listed. Yet we have bowls and water sets galore in Carnival Glass. It may have come in other colors. This marigold is the only one I have seen.

continued on page 192

SECTION 9 — NOVELTIES

Nautilus

The Little Barrel

The Insulator

The Perfume Atomizer

Seacoast Pin Tray

Sunflower Pin Tray

The Wildrose Syrup

The Town Pump

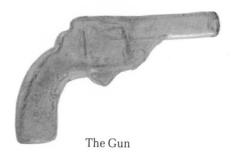

The Gun

191

continued

THE TOWN PUMP

This is one of Harry Northwood's novelties which I suspect is purely decorative. It was never made in great quantities and is one of the most sought after pieces today. Probably made in all the colors, the purple is more common than the marigold but the marigold commands the higher price as you have to go farther and search harder to find the Pump in marigold.

THE GUN

I decided to show this candy container in the novelty section because I feel that a child's toy made of glass that has survived forty or fifty years is worthy of note. Also, perhaps some of you never saw one of these in Carnival Glass so it may benefit the new collector.

These toy guns contained candy, balls or pellets. The candy balls were called Jawbreakers. That, of course, was the children's term because they were so hard.

Even a guess at the manufacturer would be impossible. This is the only color seen. In fact, it is the only gun I have seen in Carnival Glass.

THE JARDINIERE WHIMSEY

This whimsey at first looked just like some of the other Jardinieres, but some glass worker decided to make something different out of it. Maybe he got caught and his boss didn't think much of his idea, or maybe he was not too pleased with it himself, for this is the only one seen or reported to date. This Lined Thumbprint pattern was used on vases also, but is known by the name of The Diamond and Thumbprint; before the pattern is slung out, as they do the vases, there is no diamond. This has been attributed to Millersburg, which is possible. If so, then the moulds were transferred to the Fenton plant, because we saw the vases advertised after the closing of the Millersburg factory. The regular Jardiniere may be found in green, amethyst, marigold, as well as peach-opalescent.

HEAVY SWIRL PERFUME ATOMIZER

The Heavy Swirl Perfume Atomizer has been a conversation piece for many years. I contended it was Carnival, some thought it was Steuben, one well-known authority insisted that it was Imperial.

Shown beside it is a fragment of another atomizer that was discovered while digging at the Millersburg plant site. That settles it. It's Millersburg.

BEADED PANEL BUTTER DISH

The Beaded Panel Butter Dish is favored by many collectors. I have never been attracted by children's dishes and toys (purely personal) but to find something like this in mint condition prompted me to make an exception. Originally, there were other pieces in a set, possibly four.

LION'S HEAD INK WELL

The Lion's Head Ink Well is more than just a novelty. It was a practical item until the fountain pen took over. I have seen these in two other colors, red and marigold. The brass Lion leads us to suspect Fenton as the manufacturer.

COAL BUCKET

Souvenir pieces seem to attract collectors, especially if one's home town is mentioned. The coal bucket was an advertisement for a company in Rochester, New York, probably the Babcock Coal Co. The glass is good but the iridescence is only fair. The lettering is worn but legible. It probably is a product of Westmoreland.

Jardiniere Whimsey

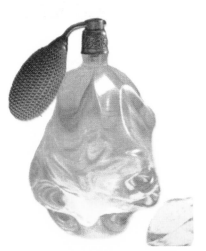

Heavy Swirl Perfume Atomizer

Beaded Panel Butter Dish

Lion's Head Ink Well

Coal Bucket

NORTHWOOD PEACOCKS PLATE

This pattern is also called Peacocks-on-the-Fence. The pronounced differences are apparent when compared with the Urn or Fountain patterns. The peacock has been a favorite pattern for many years and people at one time thought the peacock was a good omen. This pattern was used on plates and bowls and came in a variety of colors. These may or may not have the N on the bottom, but if it doesn't have, you can still be sure it is Northwood, since the Fine Rib pattern will identify the manufacturer. Shown here in amethyst, it may be found in all the colors that Northwood normally made.

HEARTS AND FLOWERS

Here is another example of fine work by Harry Northwood.

The pattern was carried over from the pressed glass days with some improvements or changes. In other words, there are differences between the pressed glass patterns and Carnival.

This was made in a variety of colors and shapes and sizes. Some pieces have the (N) mark, others don't. With or without the mark it is a lovely piece that anyone would be proud to own.

THE WINDFLOWER FLAT PLATE

This is an old pattern carried over from the pressed-glass days.

The pattern is often found in low bowls, usually marigold, occasionally a purple or a blue, but seldom found in flat plates.

I think Fenton added to this. We find the fine stippling which is typical of Fenton's products. Also, this is on beautiful cobalt glass for which Fenton was never surpassed.

HEAVY GRAPE CHOP PLATE

Chop plates today are at a premium and this one is no exception. Though some are probably more sought after than this one, it is still highly collectable. This was first attributed to Fenton and later to Imperial. Regardless of who may have been the maker, it is still worthy of a spot among the best. Shown here in a true amber, it also came in marigold, amethyst and green.

SECTION 10 — FLAT PLATES

Northwood Peacocks Plate

Hearts and Flowers Plate

Windflower Flat Plate

Heavy Grape

APPLE BLOSSOM TWIGS PLATE

We gave you a double-take on this one. These plates are just a little different. The blue is ruffled just a little and the peach-opalescent is flat. Actually there is less than ½″ difference in the heights of the two. These were made by Fenton, and he also made a lot of shallow bowls in this pattern. I suspect the bowls and plates were made from the same mould and came in all the other colors including white, but no red has been reported.

HORSE MEDALLION PLATE

This 8″ plate has almost the identical pattern found on the rose bowl, but I don't think they were made from the same mould. This plate has the Bearded Berry pattern on the back, and of course, there are no feet on the plate. This is a double rarity because flat plates with animals are rare, and this honey-amber color is rare. I have reasons to believe that Mr. Frank Fenton, senior, designed this pattern himself, and he did an excellent job on it. This may be found in cobalt blue as well as green, amethyst, marigold, and possibly white.

ROUND-UP PLATE

This pattern may have been made to compliment the cattlemen of the West. We have the cactus leaves and the old brands which were used very extensively at the time these plates were made. This was made by Fenton, and again, they made more bowls than plates, but it is thought these were rather popular. The plates can be found in marigold, blue and the peach-opalescent, as shown here, and also we have found these in a beautiful frosty white — though the latter two colors are not plentiful.

Apple Blossom Twigs Plate

Horse Medallion Plate

Round-Up Plate

PERSIAN MEDALLION PLATE

This plate with the oriental motif is one of the old standbys. Like many patterns, it is more plentiful in bowls than plates, and came in most of the colors, with marigold and blue the most common. Some of the amethyst are very nice and the white was good too. This is a Fenton piece. The one shown here is azure blue — just a trifle lighter than the cobalt blue. It may also be found in a 10" chop plate.

ACANTHUS PLATE

This is a variant of the Millersburg Whirling Leaves. This is the first piece of Millersburg that I have found that was marked other than the lettering on the souvenir pieces. Not all of these are marked, but some of these have what I suspect are the initials of the mould maker on the stem of one of the leaves. There has been some confusion as to what the letters are, but they are there, very small and hard to read. Why on some and not all, I can't explain. This pattern may be found on bowls also, and in at least three different colors — marigold, green and amethyst.

FANCIFUL PLATE

This, I think, shows Fenton at its best. It is a very simple pattern — a few leaves, some flowers and some fruit, possibly strawberries, and a little scrollwork. But clever manipulation and arranging, some neat cross-hatching in the strawberries, and stippling turned this pattern into a good piece of art work instead of just another pattern. For some reason, the bowls got the jump on the plates again, because there are far more bowls than plates. Shown here in a deep purple, it may be found in amethyst, blue, green, marigold and white.

HATTIE CHOP PLATE

Like many other of the choice pieces, this usually brings controversies as to who the maker was. I don't think anyone really knows. Some think Millersburg, others think Imperial Glass Co. Whoever made it did a nice job. This Chop Plate, like most of the others, was probably made from a large bowl and just flattened out. It probably came in most of the usual colors. It is highly collectable and desirable as are all the Chop plates, and was photographed in the Moore's home.

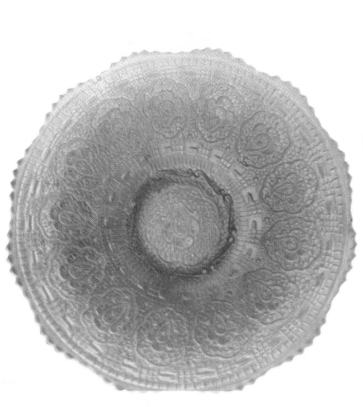

Persian Medallion Plate

Acanthus Plate

Fanciful Plate

Hattie Chop Plate

ROSE SHOW PLATE

This is probably one of Northwood's finest plates. Don't look for any marks — one look at the bottom will tell you why. The roses indented up from the bottom are enough to tell you it would be very difficult to mark. And again, we think the mould was used for both the plates and bowls — the bowls being more plentiful than the plates, and usually sell for less money. These may be found in most colors, (no peach-opalescent has been reported) but an aqua-opalescent is very scarce and very expensive.

POPPY SHOW PLATE

This is the mate to the Rose Show Plate, being almost identical except it has the Poppy pattern instead of the Rose, and the lines for the back pattern on the Poppy Show run up and down while on the Rose Show they run around the bowl. This is generally thought to be Northwood and I agree. As usual, the plates are harder to come by than the bowls. This also came in a variety of colors, perhaps white and ice-blue being more common than the ice-green, which is very scarce. I have seen this plate in an ice-green opalescent and it is very striking. It seems the collectors are evenly divided in their choice between the Rose Show and the Poppy Show, so most keep one of each.

SCALES PLATE

This plate looks like it might be peach-opalescent coloring, but it is what we call milk glass that was iridized, because some companies advertised this as "pearly edges and pearly underneath". When they advertised this as "Iridescent Art Glass", some people started calling this Pearl Carnival Glass. To simplify things, we just called it Milk Glass Carnival. Whatever you choose to call it, the plates are very hard to come by, and there are no marks to help identify the manufacturer.

ORANGE TREE PLATE

This pattern was widely used by Fenton and may have been his most popular pattern. There were water sets, table sets, bowls galore, and in many sizes, but for some reason we don't see many of these plates, and in few colors. Blue and marigold are the most common, occasionally a white, but very seldom do you see a green.

Rose Show Plate

Poppy Show Plate

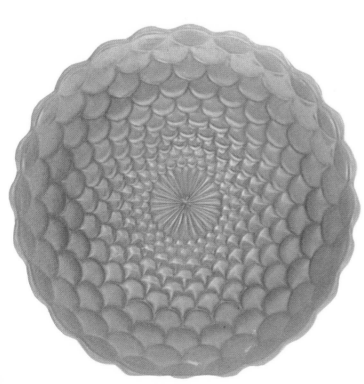

Scales Plate

Orange Tree Plate

THREE FRUITS PLATE

This plate must have been Northwood's most popular plates at the time they were made. This is the only pattern I have found in which the plates were almost as available as the bowls. These are a standard size 9″ plate, and maybe half of them have the N in the bottom. Usually the ones with the plain back have the N, while the ones with the Fine Rib pattern on the back are seldom marked. This comes in all the colors. The aqua-opalescent is the favorite color for now, at least, and it is the most expensive at the time of this writing.

COMET PLATE

This plate was made by Fenton and apparently was not used very much. We only find this pattern on plates and bowls, and not too many of either. Somehow this pattern must have fallen beside the by-way, because we don't find it very often. It comes in blue as shown here, amethyst, marigold and green. Perhaps it came in white too, though I don't recall seeing one.

ADVERTISING PIECES

This lovely dinner plate would be a collector's item even without the words, "Compliments of Spector's Department Store."

I often wonder if the head of that store ever dreamed how much value would be placed on those five little words.

The Heart and Vine design tells that this was made by Fenton Art Glass Company of Williamstown, West Virginia.

Three Fruits Plate

Comet Plate

Spector's Advertising Plate

GRAPE AND CABLE ICE BLUE OPALESCENT PLATE

The color of this plate sets it apart from a lot of the other ones. Northwood made lots of Grape and Cable plates in a wide variety of colors, but very few of the ice blue had the opalescence added. Perhaps it did not sell too well or perhaps they thought handling it one more time in the making was not worth the effort, as the opalescent was not selling that good at that time. Today it would be on the "most wanted" list.

THE GREEK KEY PLATE

This is a standard size plate, about 9″ across. Made by Northwood, some are marked with the N, others are not. The bowls seem to be more plentiful than the plates, but even the bowls are not really plentiful. It seems that most of them are green, though occasionally you will see one in amethyst or marigold. Apparently this pattern was not too popular at the time.

VINTAGE HANDLED PLATE, OR COOKIE SERVER

This plate or server is not too plentiful and my first guess would be that it is because it is hard to display or to store. However, it did have its merits. It was large, about 14″ across, and had a good sturdy handle for passing cookies, sandwiches, or what have you. Perhaps the first time the family moved, the handle got broken off. There are no identifying marks, and the Vintage pattern is of little help in knowing the maker, because every company had a grape pattern called Vintage beside their own Grape pattern.

WISHBONE FOOTED PLATE

This large footed plate was made by Northwood. The pattern was also used with different pieces such as bowls, water sets, and epergnes as well as the flat plate. This footed plate was probably made from a large bowl and made in a variety of sizes, shapes and colors. Like many other pieces and patterns made by Northwood, some were marked with the N, others were not. Marked or not, it is a desirable piece in any color.

Grape and Cable Ice Blue Opalescent Plate

Greek Key Plate

Vintage Handled Plate or Cookie Server

Wishbone Footed Plate

FENTON'S GRAPE AND CABLE FOOTED PLATE

This Grape and Cable has puzzled collectors since they started to collect Carnival Glass. Which was Fenton and which was Northwood? If you will study closely you will soon discover a difference in the grapes, and also in the leaves and the cable. If that is not enough, then look at the feet and the panels. You will see they are the same as those we find on the Stag and Holly, Fenton's Windmill and Mums, Flowers and Water Lilies, and others we know to be Fenton's.

SAILING SHIP FLAT PLATE

This plate would by no means compare with the Rose Show plate, or Persian Garden chop plate, or Fenton's Heavy Grape chop plate, but it is nice. I think most collectors would enjoy one as much as we have enjoyed ours. We don't think this is late Carnival, such as Bouquet and Lattice, and we wouldn't venture a guess at the manufacturer. We don't think it was made by one of the major companies that made so much Carnival.

NORTHWOOD'S GRAPE AND CABLE FOOTED PLATE

We have two reasons for showing this footed plate again. Many people believe it was made just in purple, so we chose this ice green. Another reason is for a quick comparison between Northwood and Fenton Grape and Cable footed plates. Northwood's must have been more popular because there are more of them, or at least we have seen more of them.

ROSE SHOW VARIANT FLAT PLATE

When you look at this one you think it is the Rose Show Plate we see all the time. On closer examination you will notice the roses are not quite as high. Then we look at the underside and find the indentations are not there, but we find the rib pattern Northwood used on Peacocks on the Fence and some of the Goodluck Bowls. We don't know how many of these there are around, but we know of two more. We feel sure it is Northwood, although unmarked.

Fentons Grape and Cable Footed Plate

The Sailing Ship Flat Plate

Northwood's Grape and Cable Footed Plate

Rose Show Variant Flat Plate

WIDE PANEL CAKE PLATE

This I believe is the largest of the flat plates; at least it is the largest I have seen in Carnival Glass. It measures 15 inches wide by 1¼ inches high and sits on a 4½ inch collar base. This has fair color and the iridescence is good. There are no identifying marks, so we wouldn't venture a guess as to the manufacturer.

PERSIAN GARDEN CHOP PLATE

This large chop plate was made by Fenton and, no doubt, was made from the large ice cream bowl from the set. We also find the small plates that were made from the small dishes that went with the ice cream set. These chop plates usually measure slightly more than 12″ across and the small ones about 6″ across. These are probably found in white more often than the other colors. The marigold is probably next, and then the amethyst, which is very beautiful. I suspect the peach-opalescent, shown here, is the hardest one to find. But any chop plate, in any color, in this pattern is a collector's find.

OPEN ROSE FLAT PLATE

There have been reissues of this pattern in several sizes and shapes, perhaps even on flat plates. The reissues are marked with an I.G. — or a "G" with an "I" running through it. The old ones are nice and well worth searching for. This was made by the Imperial Glass Company.

NORTHWOOD'S PLAIN FLAT PLATE

We don't know if this was a goof or not. I don't recall any of the Northwood pieces without a pattern, so we thought you just might enjoy this. If this had the same iridescence we find on Stretch Glass, I would say it was Stretch, but it doesn't have the Stretch effect. It is the same type of iridescence we find on all the Carnival made by Northwood. By the way, it does have the famous (N).

Wide Panel Cake Plate

Persian Garden Chop Plate

Open Rose Flat Plate

Northwood's Plain Flat Plate

SCROLL EMBOSSED FLAT PLATE

This pattern was widely used. We find it on bowls and compotes as well as flat plates. It must have been popular on small compotes. Occasionally you find a flat plate such as shown here, but not as easily as the compotes. This is thought to be an Imperial Glass product.

FISH SCALE PLATE

This small plate is not seen too often. Perhaps it was used or intended to be used for serving salted nuts or mints. Anyway, it seems there were not many made, because they are not plentiful. This plate measures from 7″ to 8″ and almost always comes in the peach-opalescent color. However, I have also seen it in an amethyst, and the way the scales pick up the beautiful iridescence, you would think they would have made a lot of these. The Wild Rose pattern on the back leads us to believe this was made by Northwood, but again, we can't be sure.

NORTHWOOD'S GOOD-LUCK PLATE

This is Northwood's version of the Good-Luck which he used very extensively on bowls as well as plates, and was made in all the colors. Probably the ice-blue is the favorite in the plates, however some of the purple run it a close second. Many pieces of the old pressed glass also had the horse-shoe and the good-luck letters, but on most of them the rest of the pattern was different.

THE CONCORD GRAPE PLATE

The grapes here hardly look like the Concord grape, but who knows what the artist had in mind when he designed this pattern. This pattern is seldom found and only on bowls and plates, and is quite hard to come by. It may have come in all colors, but the few that we have encountered have been in marigold and amethyst. I have been told this was another Fenton product, and judging from the cross-hatching over the whole pattern, I would agree that is probably right.

Fish Scale Small Flat Plate

Scroll Embossed Flat Plate

Concord Grape Plate

Northwood's Good-Luck Plate

PODS AND POSIES CHOP PLATE

This large 10½" plate rates near the top of the list of chop plates. Shown here in peach opalescent, it may be found in other colors as well, most often in marigold, amethyst and green, though even these are really not that easy to come by. In fact, most collectors think a chop plate in any pattern is a treasure. This is also known by two different names. Some call it Four Flowers, but I prefer the Pods and Posies so I don't confuse it with the Millersburg Four Flower. This is a Fenton product.

LEAF CHAIN FLAT PLATE

This Leaf-Chain plate was undoubtedly a popular plate in the hey-day of Carnival, though the plate collectors have gathered up most of them by now. At one time they were fairly plentiful, which led us to believe they had a good run. The fact that flat plates have been favorites for the collectors for many years is reason enough for them to be hard to find now. The Bearded Berry pattern on the back tells us this is Fenton.

THE COSMOS FLAT PLATE

This simple but stylized pattern is just plain enough to be intriguing. There doesn't seem to be too many of these. This is a standard size 9" plate and may be found in amethyst, usually light, and an emerald green. There may have been other colors, but I haven't seen them if there are. This is generally thought to be Millersburg, and judging from the color and the iridescence, I would agree.

HOLLY AND BERRIES PLATE

This plate is about half an inch larger than most of the others, and came in a variety of colors, I believe. Shown here in marigold, which is the most common color, it may be found in amethyst, green, white and also a beautiful red, though the red in this pattern is very rare. I have seen only one or two. This is another Fenton piece.

Pods and Posies Chop Plate

Leaf Chain Flat Plate

The Cosmos Plate

Holly and Berries Plate

NU-ART CHRYSANTHEMUM CHOP PLATE

For years this was the choice chop plate among the collectors, then some of the other chop plates took the spotlight. But this one is still rated high in the top ten chop plates. These may or may not be marked "Nu-Art". Imperial made several of these chop plates and for some reason, some were not marked. Some collectors like the ones not marked "Nu-Art" perhaps because more were marked. Some of these were made as late as 1928 they claim, but these have the color and iridescence of the best of the early Carnival glass. Like the Nu-Art Homestead plate, these have also been reproduced.

NU-ART HOMESTEAD PLATE

This is one of my favorites of the Nu-Art plates, probably because of the unique pattern here that looks so much like our old homestead with the creek running by and the ducks swimming in the water. Shown here in green, it also came in marigold, purple and white. There is also another version of the Nu-Art plates, not shown here — the Currier and Ives, which is also very attractive and quite popular.

WISH-BONE AND SPADES CHOP PLATE

This chop plate, measuring 11″ across, was undoubtedly from the same mould as the large Wish-Bone and Spades bowl. For some reason, Fenton made a lot more of the bowls than he did the plates. Shown here in deep purple, it may also be found in marigold and green, and on rare occasions, in a very striking peach-opalescent. Just which color, or even which chop plate, is really the favorite would be most difficult for any writer to decide. These are from the Moores collection.

GARDEN PATH VARIANT CHOP PLATE

This plate is so much like the Garden Path chop plate that it seems as though it was hardly worthwhile to change the mould for this pattern, but for some reason it was changed, and like the Wishbone and Spades, we believe it was the same mould used for the large bowls and flattened out. I seriously doubt that Mr. Fenton ever dreamed that one of these chop plates would ever sell for more than a thousand dollars, though I am sure he knew this was one of the finest. These perhaps came in all colors, though we have only seen them in blue, amethyst and marigold. So far, every one we have seen was exceptional in color and iridescence.

Nu-Art Chrysanthemum Chop Plate

Nu-Art Homestead Plate

Wishbone and Spades Chop Plate

Garden Path Variant Chop Plate

PEACOCK AND URN CHOP PLATE

The Peacock and Urn chop plate is quite rare. The beading on the urn tells right away it is Northwood, though this one does have the N on the bottom. This was made from the large ice-cream bowl, and bowls must have sold a lot better than plates when these were made, because they made very few of these. The collector who has one is lucky.

LITTLE FLOWERS CHOP PLATE

Bowls with this pattern are fairly common and are in most of the colors Fenton made, but the chop plate is something else. No doubt this was made from a bowl. There are so few of these plates that the source of supply can't meet the demand, so the price goes up.

STAG AND HOLLY FOOTED CHOP PLATE

This chop plate was formed from the large Stag and Holly fruit bowl, or if you prefer, the centerpiece bowl. More often seen in marigold, but on rare occasions you will find this in a cobalt blue that is very striking. We don't think these were made in large quantities, perhaps just enough to keep the collector looking. These were made by Fenton.

DRAGON AND LOTUS FLAT PLATE

This is a standard 9″ plate. We find bowls galore in this pattern, in all the colors including red, but the plates are very scarce, so the colors are also limited. I have found these only in marigold and blue, though there must be more. This must have been one of Mr. Fenton's favorite patterns and why he did not make more of the plates is a mystery.

Peacock and Urn Chop Plate

Little Flowers Chop Plate

Stag and Holly Footed Chop Plate

Dragon and Lotus Flat Plate

MILLERSBURG CHERRIES MILK PITCHER

This little milk pitcher took my eye at once. The design is hard to come by compared to more common shapes, even though it was a popular item. I found several broken pieces at Millersburg with this pattern in green, white, amethyst and marigold.

ROSE GARDEN MILK PITCHER

A most difficult piece to find. It is a good heavy glass with outstanding iridescence. Occasionally you will find a large glass with this pattern, but I don't recall ever seeing a water set with it.

FIELD THISTLE WATER PITCHER

Very similar in some ways to the Inverted Thistle, but not enough to be confusing. This one doesn't carry the nearcut mark. May also be found in purple and green. The maker is unknown.

INVERTED THISTLE WATER PITCHER

This lovely is unmarked and, like the Inverted Strawberry doesn't offer clues as to the maker. It is very transparent which is unlike Imperial or Northwood. Sets are uncommon and the pitchers alone are becoming scarce.

SECTION 11 — RARE WATER PITCHERS

Millersburg Cherries Milk Pitcher

Rose Garden Milk Pitcher

Field Thistle Water Pitcher

Inverted Thistle Water Pitcher

FROLICKING BEAR WATER PITCHER

I think I'm safe in saying that this is extremely rare. I know of three of these pitchers and one tumbler. There are numerous stories about the manufacturer of these water sets and how they were given away with 100-pound sacks of flour, but to date I have not been able to authenticate any of them. Anyway, we all agreed that this is a most desirable piece.

MAY FLOWER WATER PITCHER

This is one of the nice ones that is not too easily found, and a trifle harder to locate in dark than in marigold. And of course, the tumbler collectors take their toll, which makes it difficult to build a set. It is thought this was made by Imperial Glass.

WAFFLE BLOCK WATER PITCHER

Quite often you see Punch Bowls, Cups and Baskets, (also Vases) in this pattern — and once in awhile, a Pitcher. I don't recall ever seeing a tumbler to this set though I'm sure they were made (and possibly even in other colors). Somehow they have escaped my notice.

STRAWBERRY SCROLL WATER PITCHER

One of the more difficult water sets to find. Shown here in a beautiful blue. Though it is most difficult to find in any color, the dark is the hardest to discover. Occasionally you will find a tumbler in marigold. This was made by Fenton Glass.

Frolicking Bear Water Pitcher

May Flower Water Pitcher

Waffle Block Water Pitcher

Strawberry Scroll Water Pitcher

INVERTED STRAWBERRY WATER PITCHER

We have shown this pattern in another shape, but due to so many inquiries, we show it again in this pitcher. May be found also in amethyst or green. From the Schleede's.

GRAPEVINE LATTICE WATER PITCHER

The set shown is a little more scarce than the Grape and Lattice displayed on one of our other books, however, it may still be found. This we feel sure is a Fenton product. There were six matching tumblers not shown. Our thanks to Robert Neroni for lending this piece.

MARILYN WATER PITCHER

This is one of the Millersburg near-cut patterns that always catch the collector's eye. The color doesn't seem to matter, as long as it is the Marilyn. It is desirable whether it is a pitcher, a tumbler or the whole set. Possibly the amethyst has a slight lead as to color. This came in green too, but you don't see any blue. Perhaps it only came in the three colors.

INVERTED FEATHER MILK PITCHER

There doesn't seem to be much information available about this one. We are accustomed to seeing this pattern on the cracker jar and, shown elsewhere in the book, in the punchbowl. This pitcher is rather small for a water pitcher, and large for a milk pitcher, and no tumblers have been reported. Whether it's a milk pitcher or water pitcher makes little difference, as it is the only one I have seen, and I think it is quite rare. This is in the Moore's collection.

Inverted Strawberry Water Pitcher

Grapevine Lattice Water Pitcher

Marilyn Water Pitcher

Inverted Feather Milk Pitcher

223

RISING SUN WATER PITCHER

Few people would have trouble identifying this rare pitcher with the sun just starting to climb the horizon. These seem to be in limited supply. There is another type with the pitcher having a pedestal foot. One was found with the six matching tumblers, and also one in blue with six tumblers. Some people think these might be English, others think they were made by Jenkins Glass Works. Whoever made them did a nice job, and he who finds one is fortunate, as were the Moore's.

STAR-FLOWER WATER PITCHER

This rare water pitcher, shown here in blue, is so attractive you would think they would have made loads of them, but for some reason they are just not to be had. We have seen it only in blue, and one general opinion is that it is an unmarked Northwood piece which is highly possible, because Northwood marked the tumblers and not the pitchers. We have found no tumblers so we can't confirm this is a Northwood piece.

GRAPE AND CABLE TANKARD PITCHER

Northwood made several tankard water pitchers other than the Grape and Cable but few would cause more excitement at an auction than this one in ice green. The Grape and Cable tankards are scarce in any color. This is another set that is hard to put together because tumbler collectors are after these tumblers. The tumblers that go with this set are taller and flare out a little at the top, so it is fairly easy for the collectors to recognize them and at a show or shop they don't stay long. The fortunate owners are Moore's.

FASHION WATER PITCHER AND CREAMER

It is a pleasure indeed to show this water pitcher and the little creamer in purple in the rare section. I suspect the water pitcher is more rare than the creamer, but both are most difficult to obtain. The two pictured are from the collection of Don and Connie Moore. These were made by the Imperial Glass Company, which made some of the finest pieces in purple. We wonder now why they did not make more of the purple, but at that time marigold was the important color.

Rising Sun Water Pitcher

Star-Flower Water Pitcher

Grape and Cable Tankard Pitcher

Fashion Water Pitcher and Creamer

GREEK KEY WATER PITCHER

This is another one of the water sets that is often hard to get together with the pitcher collectors and the tumbler collectors after each. This one came in all the colors. The amethyst probably was the easiest to find, the green next and the marigold trailing. The white, the ice blue and the ice green are nearly impossible to find. Plates and bowls may also be found with this pattern and may or may not have the N mark, but we are confident it is a Northwood product.

WISHBONE WATER PITCHER

It is easy to see why this set is so desirable. It is not easy to obtain one and you wonder why there were not a lot more of these made. This must have been a popular pattern because we find it on bowls, plates and epergnes, in all colors including the peach-opalescent chop plate. No water sets have been reported in the peach-opalescent color. Most of the pieces carry the N mark.

PERFECTION WATER PITCHER

This is another one of the more desirable water sets which is definitely scarce. For some reason it seems as though this was never produced in great quantities. Because the pitcher and the tumblers are both highly desirable, the pitcher collectors are after the pitchers, and the tumbler collectors are after the tumblers, so it is difficult to acquire a complete set. This set has been attributed to Northwood. Personally, I disagree, and think it is a toss-up between Millersburg and Fenton. It seems to have come in all the usual colors.

COSMOS AND CANE PITCHER

The tankard type pitchers seem to catch the collector's eye, and this one is no exception. Some of the tumblers were advertising pieces, but not all of them. I don't recall any of the pitchers with any lettering on them, though it is possible. What few of these I have seen were white, occasionally a marigold. You may find this pattern on table sets and occasionally bowls, but somehow you don't find a lot of this pattern on any pieces. The maker is unknown.

Greek Key Water Pitcher

Wishbone Pitcher

Perfection Water Pitcher

Cosmos and Cane Pitcher

ORANGE TREE ORCHARD WATER PITCHER

Here is another one of the Orange Tree patterns by Fenton, though this one was never used to the extent that the regular Orange Tree was. It was used mostly for water sets. This set is quite scarce, especially in white. Your chances of finding it in blue or marigold are much better.

HOBSTAR BAND PEDESTAL FOOT WATER PITCHER

I hardly believed this when I saw it — a pedestal foot on this pitcher. I think it is quite unusual. Whether it is worth more or less, I would not venture a guess, but it is different. This is the only one I have seen. Chances are there are more of these and in other colors.

FENTONIA WATER PITCHER

This is one of the most desirable of the water sets that Fenton made, however it seems that this was a very limited production. This pattern was also used on berry sets, but sparingly. Possibly it came in all the colors, but marigold is found more readily, and the blue is more difficult. It probably came in green also, but I don't recall seeing one in green.

Orange Tree Orchard Pitcher

Hob Star Band Pedestal Pitcher

Fentonia Water Pitcher

GRAPE AND CABLE FERNERY

The Grape and Cable fenery is always in demand regardless of the color. Probably ice-blue leads pricewise, but the marigold, shown here, is very close behind. We wonder why Northwood didn't make a lot more of these, though in the last ten years many more have shown up than we ever thought existed. One was found with the original liner. There are not nearly enough for each collector to have one of these.

(NOTE the little inset. The price has changed considerably).

IRIDESCENT GLASS FERN DISH.

AO2144—Iridescent grape pattern, claw foot, height 4¼ inches, width 8 inches, perforated enameled white liner; 2 doz. in barrel....doz., **$6.50**

Less than barrel, each, **60c**

IRIDESCENT FERN DISH.

AO2112—Size 6½x3½ inches, footed, with glass perforated liner, raised grape pattern; assorted colors, golden iris, wine ruby and royal blue iridescent effect; total, 3 doz. in barrel....doz., **$1.95**

Less than barrel, doz., **$2.20**

(VINTAGE NUT DISH)

SMALL FERN DISH

This small fern dish has caused much confusion. Many times advertised as Grape and Cable Fernery, which is wrong. It is not Grape and Cable — it is a Vintage pattern and has no Cable, was not made by Northwood and is far less desirable unless you happen to find it in red. Even then it would be worth far less than the Grape and Cable Fernery — in any color. This is a nice, desirable piece, but should not be mistaken for the Grape and Cable Fernery. Made in the usual colors including cobalt blue.

HOLLY WHIRL WHIMSEY

I think this little candy dish is quite different from most of the whimseys as they usually add something instead of taking it away. This time they left the handle off the sauce-boat and reshaped it into a round dish, crimped the edges, and came up with a beautiful candy dish. This was made by Millersburg. I have seen only this one and this color, though other colors or pieces are possible.

GRAPE AND CABLE BON-BON

The bon-bons are still desirable but not quite the rage they were ten or more years ago. They are a must for most collections, and this is one of the favorites, usually priced rather modestly. Almost all of these have the N marked on the bottom, but if it didn't have the N, you would recognize Northwood by the Cable, anyway. These are found in amethyst, marigold, blue, green, occasionally white, or maybe pastel colors.

GRAPE AND CABLE BANANA BOAT

The Grape and Cable Banana Boat is another one of the controversial pieces. Many people think they are not Northwood's because they don't have the N on them. I think they are Northwood's because of the ice-blue and the ice-green colors. I don't know of another company that made the ice-blue and ice-green that looks anywhere close to the Northwood colors. We find these listed in the old catalogs as "oval Orange bowls". Occasionally you will find one of these with a band around the top which is a variant Grape and Cable pattern. These came in all the colors that Northwood made.

Grape and Cable Fernery

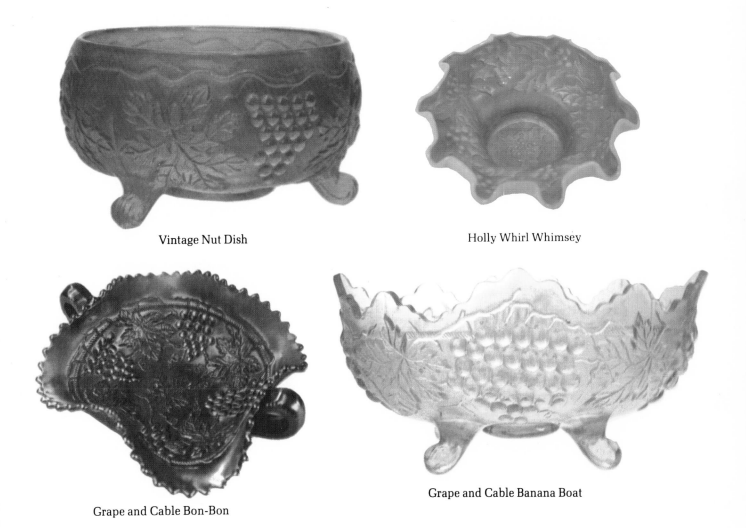

Vintage Nut Dish

Holly Whirl Whimsey

Grape and Cable Bon-Bon

Grape and Cable Banana Boat

THE LADIES SWIRL-HOBNAIL CUSPIDOR

These must have been designed with a beautiful lady in mind for they are so nice and dainty. I think these were taken from the rose-bowl mould. If you will notice, you can see a ring where the tool was used to squeeze it in below the top, then it was flared out to form the flat top. Most of them have the hobnails flattened out just above where the tool left the ring. Amethyst and marigold are the colors usually found, however I did dig up about a quarter of one of these in green at the old Millersburg plant, so we know they attempted to make at least one in green.

RIB AND PANEL CUSPIDOR

This cuspidor, like most of the others, was fashioned from a vase and shaped to suit the glass worker's fancy. This one is 4 inches high and 6½" at the widest point. Some may be a little bit more flared and the top flattened down more, though I don't think these were ever made in a large quantity. Almost all the companies had some kind of rib pattern, so there is little chance to identify the maker of this piece.

BUTTERFLY AND BERRY CUSPIDOR

Most of the cuspidors were made from a piece intended for an entirely different use, and this one is no exception. This was made from the sugar bowl of the four-piece table set. Again we can't be sure how many of these are to be found, but from all indications, there are very few. The four-piece table set was made in about all the colors Fenton made except possibly red, but the blue shown here is the only cuspidor I have seen or had reported. Our thanks to the Moores.

COUNTRY KITCHEN CUSPIDOR

Rare indeed is this cuspidor — could be one of a kind. At the present time it is the only one we know of. Some glass worker shaped this from a spooner to his personal liking. We often refer to these pieces as "whimseys". One look at the color and iridescence and you would know it was a Millersburg piece, even if you did not know this was a Millersburg pattern. The four-piece table setting in the Country Kitchen pattern is scarce, and may yet be found, but I'm not so sure about finding another one of these. Our thanks to the Whitleys for the loan of this piece.

IMPERIAL GRAPE CUSPIDOR

This cuspidor was probably made from a small bowl. It measures 5¾" at the widest point, has a 3" base and is 3¼" high — much larger than the Grape and Cable cuspidor. Imperial made several berry sets and several occasional bowls so we think one of the workers made this on his own and not in any quantity. I think most glass workers did this every so often. This I would class as a whimsey — something made to suit the worker's whim or taste. Thanks to the Tiltons for this piece.

The Ladies Swirl-Hobnail Cuspidor

Rib and Panel Cuspidor

Butterfly and Berry Cuspidor

Imperial Grape Cuspidor

Country Kitchen Cuspidor

LUSTER-ROSE LARGE FRUIT BOWL

This is one of the largest pieces you will find in red, with the exception of the Gone-With-the-Wind lamps. Though other companies made some large bowls, they were not quite this massive and many of the large bowls did not have the good color all the way through. This is one of the finest specimens of red we have encountered. Imperial Glass Company made many of these in other colors — marigold, clambroth, purple, blue, green and smoke, but apparently very few in red.

BUTTERFLY AND TULIP SQUARE BOWL

The butterfly has always been a favorite pattern for many people, though you seldom see one this massive, covering the whole flower. We think this square type bowl does a little something else for this pattern, as it lets the butterfly spread his wings a little more. This piece may be found in marigold and green as well as in amethyst, as shown here. Also, you are more likely to find it in another shape — a deep oval or sometimes almost round, but the flat square one shown here is the most difficult to find. There are no identifying marks, but we think it is a Northwood product.

MILLERSBURG HEAVY GRAPE BOWL

This Heavy Grape is far different from the other well known Heavy Grape pieces we have seen. The color and the iridescence is almost unbelievable. This is a large shallow bowl 10" wide. There may have been smaller bowls that went with this though I don't recall ever seeing any. Our thanks to the Moores for the use of this piece.

Luster-Rose
Large Fruit Bowl

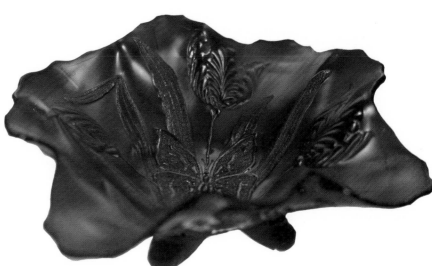

Butterfly and Tulip
Square Bowl

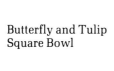

Millersburg
Heavy Grape Bowl

BIRMINGHAM AGE HERALD PLATE

Even in some areas today, our paper boys bring around a calendar at Christmas, with their greetings, for which we usually give them a couple of dollars tip. I wonder how much of a tip people gave the paperboys who passed out these plates! I am sure they were not as generous then as we would be now. Apparently many people did not appreciate these plates too much, because few kept them. The "Age Herald" was a large newspaper and had thousands of customers, but few of the plates and bowls survived. Many people think these were made by Fenton.

GODDESS OF HARVEST BOWL

This bowl is very rare, I believe, and the debate goes on as to whether it is Fenton or Millersburg. I have seen only a couple of these and they were about the same size — about 9″ wide with a ribbon-candy edge, one in amethyst like the one shown, and one in marigold. Actually there are not enough around to get any trace of them, and no marks to identify the manufacturer. But regardless of who might have made them, it is a lovely piece and most any collector would be thrilled to find one.

LITTLE FLOWERS AMBERINA BOWL

Fenton made lots of bowls with this pattern and some chop plates, but probably not too many with this amberina coloring. Actually this looks more like Art Glass than Carnival Glass. It is about a 10″ bowl and highly desirable. How many of these are around I don't know. I have seen one other — it sold at an auction near the thousand dollar mark. This one is in the Moore's collection.

Birmingham Age
Herald Plate

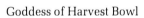
Goddess of Harvest Bowl

Little Flowers
Amberina Bowl

CHRISTMAS COMPOTE

This is perhaps the most sought after compote of any, and we can see why, for several reasons. First, all of these I have seen had exceptionally good color and iridescence. It is shaped very gracefully and the holly leaves spaced just right as they wind around the sides to catch the light and reflect the iridescence. Perhaps the size has something to do with it, too, though they vary some in size, because they were shaped partly by hand. They average about 9½" across the top and about 5" inches high. We have seen these in green and purple and marigold, possibly was made in other colors, but there are so few of these around that it is doubtful. This is Millersburg at its finest.

MULTIFRUITS AND FLOWERS COMPOTE

This compote, I believe, was made from the base of the Multifruits punch-bowl, which required a small amount of work while the glass was still hot. I don't believe these were made in a mass amount, else there would be more of them available. These were made by Millersburg and possibly came in other colors. I have seen only two of these and they were both amethyst.

LARGE CORN VASE

Apparently Mr. Northwood made three tries before he came up with a mould that was successful for the Corn vase. This is one of them. Another one had a bee on it. I believe the other one was similar to this only the husks protruded out a little more than this one does. It caused more trouble getting the piece out of the mould and the breakage was so great that it just was not feasible to use this mould. Otherwise they might have all been like this one. Here it is shown in amethyst. It is 7" inches high and 4" inches across. Yes, this one does have the N in the bottom. After this, we think he designed the smaller one where the husks didn't protrude out so far and was easier to remove from the mould. This one belongs to the Moore's.

WHIMSEY HAT PIN HOLDER

We think the artist or glass worker had a hat-pin holder in mind when he shaped this unique piece. This piece was made from a small vase. The vases with this pattern are usually referred to as Diamond and Thumbprint, but this looks more like the jardiniere, the same pattern, but not stretched out. This pattern has been attributed to Millersburg, but I have always thought it was a toss-up between Millersburg and Fenton. In either case, I am sure you will agree it is quite a unique piece and would enhance any collection. Our thanks to the Whitley's.

Christmas Compote

Multifruits and Flowers Compote

Large Corn Vase

Whimsey
Hatpin
Holder

THE PEOPLES VASE

This rare and beautiful vase is unusual in the Carnival glass field, not because of its size or its shape, but because of its motif. There are three separate sets of people each doing different things, which tells a story. The legend of this particular piece was that it was made to compliment the Amish people, who had contributed much to the Millersburg Glass Co. Whether or not this is true, to date, I have been able only to determine that these vases were made at Millersburg, and very few are to be found. We chose this one for the reason that it is shaped differently — this one has a slightly flared top which sets it aside from the other ones. Our grateful thanks to the Whitley's, who have contributed much toward this book and the advancement of Carnival glass.

THE ELK PAPERWEIGHT

Collectors have collected paperweights long before Carnival Glass, but few paperweights cause more excitement than this Elk paperweight when offered for sale at an auction or show. This is a souvenir piece from one of the Elk's Club gala events — likely a convention. These are believed to have been made by Millersburg and are all highly desirable.

CLEVELAND MEMORIAL ASH TRAY

Just how many of these were made is anybodys guess, but many people wish there had been more, or that more had survived. However, you would think from the amount of work and the fine detail that went into the making of this mould, that they would have made a lot of them. This is believed to be a souvenir piece for some gala event and were given away. Perhaps that is the reason more didn't survive, yet you would think that anything this beautiful would have had tender loving care. This is one of Millersburg's finest examples. All we have seen were dark amethyst and the finest iridescence. Our thanks to Don and Connie Moore.

The Elk Paperweight

The Peoples Vase

Cleveland Ash Tray

COSMOS LAMP

This little fellow would set any lamp collector's heart to throbbing. It is slightly over 8 inches high and about a 5 inch shade. It has good color and good iridescence. This pattern is far different than the Cosmos and Cane, so we can rule that out. Several companies made a Cosmos pattern so we have little chance of ever identifying the maker of this lamp, but I think that is of small importance. They surely made more of these. Maybe that small shop you passed up or the one you will find tomorrow might have just such a treasure as this. Our thanks to the Bruns for the loan of this beautiful piece.

THE FISH VASE

This medium sized vase is quite unusual. It is 9½" high and 3½" in diameter at the widest point. There are no marks to identify the company who made it, and the maker is quite controversial. Some think it is English and about an equal number think it is Jenkins. Regardless of who made it, this is an attractive piece and quite different, and was provided by the Moore's. ·

NORTHWOOD DRAPE TABLE LAMP

Though we have seen these shades before, the lamp itself is so much different than we usually see that I wanted to share this with you. I think the over-all effect of this lamp is very striking. I don't know who made the metal base and other parts of the lamp — Northwood made the shades. I would like to thank the lady that loaned this piece though I am unable to use her name.

THE TOMAHAWK

Candy containers are highly collectable today, but I can't think of one that could compare with this little prize that came in one of the candy containers. Many of these tomahawks, or hatchets, came in the buckets of Christmas hard-candy, though most of these were not iridized. I remember seeing some, but they were just clear glass. I believe there was ten pounds of candy in the wooden bucket. The store-keeper, many times, opened the buckets and sold the candy a penny's-worth or a nickle's-worth, and of course, gave the hatchet to the lucky kid that happened to come in at the right time. A guess at the manufacturer would be pure conjecture. Again our thanks to the Whitley's for the loan of such a rare and lovely piece.

Cosmos Lamp

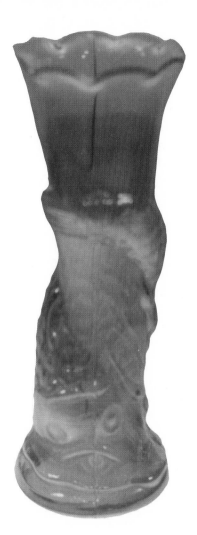

The Fish Vase

The Tomahawk

Northwood Drape Table Lamp

MULTI-FRUITS AND FLOWERS WATER PITCHER

I just wish space permitted the whole story about this water pitcher, but here is a condensed version of it. The original owner of this water pitcher was a stock boy at the Millersburg Glass Co. and when the company went into bankruptcy this water pitcher was one of the pieces from a wagon load of glass he received for his back pay. At that time the wages were low. The glass workers got a dollar and a half a day for a twelve hour shift, and he surely got less. He must have been badly disappointed when he got paid off in glass. Had he known that one pitcher alone would one day sell for more than five thousand dollars, he might have felt better. Unfortunately, we don't know if there were any tumblers in with this pitcher. If so, they could have been some of the pieces that were placed on fence posts and used for target practice with sling-shots. We just don't know, but we do know that such an extreme rarity today would bring a big buck on the market. The pitchers may be found in amethyst and possibly in green. Our appreciation goes to the Roebucks for the use of this rare pitcher.

MORNING-GLORY PITCHER

This is one of the top rarities in water pitchers and must be very hard to find. Very few of these are known and very few tumblers — no complete sets have been reported. These, I feel sure, were made by Northwood, and my first guess is that they had trouble with the mould of this one or else there would have been many more of these today. So, at the time of this writing, this is highly desirable and lucky is the collector who has one — or even one of the tumblers.

HOBNAIL WATER PITCHER

The Hobnail pitcher is one of the toughest ones to find, though at one time it must have been one of the favorite patterns. Before the Carnival Glass fad, we found the Hobnail pitchers and tumblers in the old pressed glass in clear blue, green, amber and also in the opalescent, and in many pieces other than water sets. Somehow they chose to limit the amount in Carnival, especially the water sets. Probably the blue is favored over the marigold, but I have seen more blue than marigold. I never saw a mark on a pitcher or a tumbler, but I don't think there is any doubt that these were made by Northwood.

Multifruits and Flowers Water Pitcher

Morning Glory Pitcher

Hobnail Water Pitcher Blue

Hobnail Water Pitcher Marigold

GODDESS OF ATHENA EPERGNE

The Epergne shown is much different from the ones we usually see. It is large (about 25″ tall) but it can readily be taken apart for moving. It has good heavy glass and good iridescence. There are no marks to identify the maker.

THE CHRISTMAS TREE BOTTLE

I think this is one of the most interesting bottles I have encountered. Unfortunately, the stopper had been broken, but we did have the artist make a sketch of the stopper from memory of it. This bottle is about 9″ high and about 6″ wide at the bottom. It is a good frosty white and the iridescence is very good. There are no marks to indicate who may have made this bottle. It would enhance any collection, I am sure. Our thanks to the Tilton's for the opportunity to photograph this bottle.

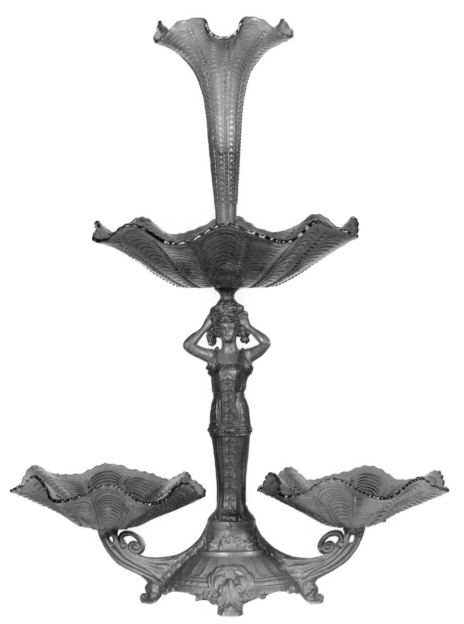

Goddess of Athena Epergne

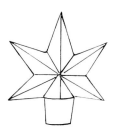

Stopper to the Christmas
Tree Bottle

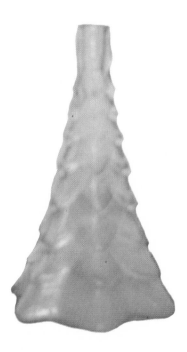

The Christmas Tree Bottle

LINED LATTICE VASE

This vase would be almost common except for the color. For some reason we don't find many of the peach-opalescent vases. However, this is one of the choice patterns in the small vases. Most of these vases average 9″-10″, this one is only 5″ high. These came in all the colors. Many people think it was made by Northwood though I have not seen one that was marked.

BUD VASE AND HOLDER

This little bud vase in the metal holder is quite unique, I think. Whether the vase was made for the holder or vise-versa, the holder is a convenient way to carry the vase without spilling the water. I would not care to venture a guess as to who may have assembled this set.

PERSIAN GARDEN WHIMSEY VASE

Perhaps the glass workers had discussed the possibilities of the base to the Persian Garden two-piece fruit bowl being used as a vase so one of the workers fashioned this one. The bottom of this base fits the bowl but the flames around the top are different heights, so it would not sit level. This was made at the Fenton factory.

PASTEL SWANS

Some think these were used as a master salt-dip. I disagree. I think they were purely decorative. Shown here are the most difficult ones to find — the purple and the peach-opalescent. They also came in blue, green, and pink. Imperial made some new ones in white, but they are enough different that I think a novice collector could tell them apart, even if they did not have the I.G. on the bottom.

KITTENS CUP AND SAUCER

Children's dishes are always fun to collect and double the fun when in Carnival Glass. We have heard all sorts of stories as to the use of these pieces and we don't believe any of them. We think they were made for children to use. These were made by Fenton and the marigold is the easiest color to find. The blue is scarce and the green is almost impossible to find.

HOBSTAR PICKLE CASTOR

This Pickle Castor can be classed as rare or scarce, either way you like. But the fact remains, there are very few of them, mainly because we were moving out of that era when Imperial Glass Company made this. They had made some of these in what we refer to as Pressed glass, which was not iridized. I have seen these in clear and a pink that were not iridized.

Lined Lattice Vase

Bud Vase and Holder

Pastel Swans

Persian Garden
Whimsey Vase

Hobstar Pickle Castor

Kittens Cup and Saucer

MILLERSBURG 4-FLOWER MINIATURE COMPOTE

We see a miniature compote now and then, and lots of middle-size ones, but this little 4-flower of Millersburg, I think is worthy of note. Probably came in the standard colors, for as you know, most everything made by Millersburg Glass was made in amethyst, green, and marigold. Thanks to the Ripley's.

FRUITS AND BERRIES COVERED BEAN POT

This large covered dish may, or may not have been used as a bean pot, but the size is just about right. It is about 10" across and 8" high — and very intriguing. The maker is unknown.

DREIBUS PARFAIT SWEETS HANDGRIP PLATE

Advertising pieces have always been collector's items; it is no surprise to find it so in Carnival Glass. This one doesn't have a visible maker's mark, but we think it was made by Northwood.

LION'S BOWL

This is one of the most popular animal dishes and not as expensive as the Peter Rabbit bowl. For some reason, this was mostly confined to small bowls and most of them are marigold. The blue is rather hard to locate and some were flattened out for plates. They are very scarce in any color, and I am sure the price would reflect that should you find one offered for sale. This was made by Fenton, who made most of our animal patterns.

MILLERSBURG CHERRIES SMALL PLATE

This is another one of the plates that was flattened out from the bowl, and in all probability was not done in a large quantity, because you just don't see these. This is the first and only one I have seen. Our thanks to the Moore's for the loan of this piece.

EXCHANGE BANK ADVERTISING PLATE

Ever since collectors have been collecting the advertising pieces have been one of their favorites, so it is understandable that it would be even more so in Carnival Glass. As for the manufacturers that made the advertising pieces, almost all of the companies did. Just remember, at that time the competition was high and nobody passed up a job. On some of the Northwood advertising pieces they sometimes used the back mould for economy and it might have had the N on it. Other than that, I don't think they were marked. Sometimes the company might use a pattern or part of a pattern we might recognize and give us a clue to who made it.

Millersburg Four Flower Miniature
Compote

Fruits and Berries
Covered Bean Pot

Dreibus Parfait Sweets
Hand Grip Plate

Lion's Bowl

Millersburg Cherries Small Plate

Exchange Bank Advertising Plate

PICTURE FRAME

This large picture frame is approximately 9×9″ and is a beautiful deep purple with outstanding iridescence. I would think that this frame would take away from most any picture. Maker unknown.

CAMBRIDGE COLOGNE BOTTLE

It pleases me no end to find a bottle on which there is no controversy about what originally came in it and its intended use as well as who made it. The experts all agree this was made by Cambridge and it was a cologne bottle. Shown here in green but I have seen this in a deep marigold that was very striking. Quite possibly this was also made in amethyst and white. As many of us know, Cambridge made many of the containers for candy, perfume, cologne and astringent. It is really no surprise they made something as graceful as this Cologne bottle.

BUZZ SAW CRUETS

I suppose almost everyone has his favorite story that someone has related to him about what originally came in these cruets, and most are different — some say liquor, some vinegar. As they came in two different sizes, I would suspect the larger size, shown here, held cologne and the smaller size, not shown, held perfume. Of the two shown here, the green one is harder to find, while the marigold and the smaller size green one are the usual ones available. This being a commercial item, there is not much way to trace the manufacturer, but the near-cut pattern leads us to believe it to be Cambridge.

STAR PAPERWEIGHT

Paperweights have always been collectible. Why there weren't more made in Carnival Glass we don't know, and what few there are around are most difficult to trace. Maker unknown.

OWL PIN

This little fellow is one of the nice ones of the small pieces. The mould-maker had his chance here, and he surely proved his skill. The maker is unknown. This piece was through the courtesy of Mr. and Mrs. Sam Wolfe of Fowler, Indiana.

KITTENS MINIATURE CUSPIDOR

I feel certain you will enjoy this little cuspidor, especially the ones who like children's pieces. It is 2½″ wide and 2″ high and was no doubt made from the little cereal bowl, or perhaps they left the handle off the cup and shaped this. However whichway it was made, there should have been more of them, because I think this is extremely rare. Our thanks to Audree Pollock of Pittsburg, Pennsylvania.

Picture Frame

Cambridge Cologne Bottle

Buzz Saw Cruets

Star Paperweight

Owl Pin

Kittens Miniature Cuspidor

INDEX